It is a commonplace that prayer is possibly the most difficult discipline of the Christian life for a pastor to maintain. Busyness of ministry, the hurry-scurry of our culture, the inundation of social media, along with our Enemy's recognition of the vital place that prayer occupies in the advance of the kingdom of the Lord Jesus, make any sincere attempt at being a prayerful pastor a battleground. This book, because it is so grounded in the Scriptures and the experience of the pastorate, is therefore welcome. Like a desert traveler coming upon a well-placed spring of water, drink in the wealth of timely insight and wisdom here!

> *Michael Haykin, professor of church history and*
> *biblical spirituality and director of The Andrew*
> *Fuller Center for Baptist Studies at The Southern*
> *Baptist Theological Seminary*

This is a little gem of a book, and smaller books may have a great impact. All believers know we should pray more and desire to pray more. Brian Croft and Ryan Fullerton, two veteran pastors, stoke the fires of prayer by showing us from the Scriptures the centrality of prayer. Prayer reveals our trust in and desperation for God. We are also given concrete practical advice on prayer. This book is convicting and encouraging and deserves a wide reading.

> *Thomas R. Schreiner, James Buchanan Harrison*
> *Professor of New Testament Interpretation and*
> *professor of biblical theology at The Southern*
> *Baptist Theological Seminary*

As pastors, we cannot change the hearts of the people we shepherd. But God can. God has called us to talk to him about them. He has chosen to use our prayers to accomplish mighty changes in the lives of those in our churches. In this book, Brian Croft and Ryan Fullerton challenge, encourage, and instruct pastors to energetically engage in the privilege and responsibility to pray for the people in our churches.

John Crotts, pastor of Faith Bible Church in Sharpsburg, Georgia, and author of Loving the Church: God's People Flourishing in God's Family

PRAY FOR THE FLOCK

PRAY FOR THE FLOCK

**Ministering God's Grace
Through Intercession**

BRIAN CROFT
AND RYAN FULLERTON

ZONDERVAN

Pray for the Flock
Copyright © 2015 by Brian Croft and Ryan Fullerton

This title is also available as a Zondervan ebook.
Visit www.zondervan.com/ebooks.

Requests for information should be addressed to:

Zondervan, 3900 *Sparks Dr. SE, Grand Rapids, Michigan 49546*

Library of Congress Cataloging-in-Publication Data

    Pray for the flock : ministering God's grace through intercession / Brian
Croft and Ryan Fullerton.
       pages cm—(Practical shepherding series)
    Includes bibliographical references
    ISBN 978-0-310-51937-9 (softcover)
    1. Intercessory prayer—Christianity. 2. Pastoral care. I. Croft, Brian,
author. II. Fullerton, Ryan, 1974- author.
BV215.P75 2015
248.3'2—dc23   2015006626

Cover design and illustrations: Jay Smith-Juicebox Designs
Interior design: Matthew Van Zomeren

Printed in the United States of America

15 16 17 18 19 20 21 22 /QG/ 20 19 18 17 16 15 14 13 12 11 10 9 8 7 6 5 4 3 2 1

Ryan: To my beloved, Christy,
who prays with "the gift of faith"

Brian: To my beloved, Cara, who prays with a
deep sincerity I long to one day experience

CONTENTS

FOREWORD

PEOPLE KNOW WHAT a doctor does. Because they can see and feel the benefits of a medical professional's work, they are willing to pay a doctor well for the services provided. People know what a mechanic generally does, as well as a plumber, a flight attendant, a salesman, and a teacher.

But much of a pastor's work is unseen. Even those laypeople closest to their pastor often do not know the basic contours of his day beyond sermon preparation and some counseling. You know your pastor works long hours; are you confident you can describe how most of them are spent? Probably not.

Yes, sermon preparation usually receives the largest share of a pastor's time during the week. Even here, the time required may surprise those most aware of their pastor's schedule. Many presume that because of their pastor's knowledge of the Bible and giftedness in public speaking, preparing to preach is quick and simple work. The truth is, men devoted to the expository preaching of God's word commonly devote fifteen to twenty hours or more each week to this task.

At the same time, God's shepherds not only feed his sheep; they also protect them through prayer. Faithful pastors, away from the eyes of the flock, often spend much time interceding for them before the Father. Here they pour out their souls for Christ to be formed in each member of the flock (Galatians 4:19) and to "present everyone fully mature in

Christ" (Colossians 1:28). Here they weep over the backslidden, grieve about conflict, cry out for God's blessing on the church, and plead for the salvation of the lost.

The kind of pastor Jesus described as "the hired hand" and "not the shepherd" (John 10:12) may do the necessary public work of ministry and get a paycheck, but true shepherds love God's flock. True shepherds love the flock when present with them, and they love the flock when present with no one but God. And one of the ways they show this love is by bringing their needs — known and unknown, tangible and spiritual, individual and congregational — to Jesus the Good Shepherd in prayer. Thus do the two pastors who have authored this book, my friends Brian Croft and Ryan Fullerton. And so we know that faithful pastors pray for the flock, but what, exactly, do they pray? Or better, what should they pray? *Pray for the Flock* helps answer that question.

This book is essentially a pastoral theology of prayer. Divided into two sections, it is a blend of both the theological and practical aspects of praying for God's people. It will provide you with biblical instruction on prayer, as well as help you organize pastoral praying rather than pray randomly about the flock. Those new to or preparing for pastoral ministry will find it particularly helpful.

In short, *Pray for the Flock*, written by two praying pastors, will teach you about praying for God's people. If you are in pastoral ministry, you'll want to consider this book. If you are a church member, consider giving this book to your pastor. Anyone should feel blessed to know that a pastor was praying for him or her in these ways. I know I do.

Don Whitney

INTRODUCTION
Brian Croft

PRAYER IS THE most difficult aspect of pastoral ministry to maintain. When I became a senior pastor, my life and ministry suddenly became very busy—busier than they had ever been before. I knew what I was *called* to do. I knew what I *should* be doing. Yet week after week, I saw the things I was supposed to do getting squeezed out of my schedule because of urgent demands on my time. And the one task that seemed to get squeezed out the most was prayer.

I'm not alone in struggling with this. Prayer requires time. And prayer is typically most fruitful when done in a quiet place, without interruptions or distractions. But the prayer needs of people probably aren't filling up your schedule. If you fail to pray, no one will notice. And making time to pray requires intentionality and planning. So in the midst of ministry, with people who want your time and attention and with many urgent tasks to complete, it's easy to neglect spending time in prayer.

A pastor knows he will be preaching every seven days, regardless of how busy the rest of his schedule gets. The sermon must get done, so time is set aside for that. And there are sick people in the hospital, and their suffering can't be ignored. These priorities weigh on your conscience, so that even if you are busy, you'll eventually make the time for them. People die unexpectedly, and a pastor is at the mercy of the family and funeral home as they make plans. Church staff meetings, meetings with elders and deacons, and other committee meetings get planned in advance, and these become default priorities in a pastor's schedule. As a pastor, you can't skip a meeting, because other people are depending on you to be there and give leadership.

But prayer isn't like any of these.

Prayer may weigh on your conscience, but there are no reminders, no complaints. Those who are not prayed for aren't aware they are forgotten. Prayer requests stay on the task list for the day, but they easily get passed over as you address more pressing demands. Many pastors, myself included, can go week after week neglecting prayer for the church. We hear a soft voice reminding us at first, until eventually the voice just fades away, drowned out by the noise of a busy life and ministry. If enough time passes, these reminders—and even the desire we have to pray—may eventually go away. Ironically, a pastor can be so busy striving to care for his people that he never makes time to stop to pray for them.

We know this is wrong. Prayerlessness reveals our lack of faith and highlights our misplaced priorities. In fact, the aim of this book is to turn up the volume knob so you will hear that soft voice speaking to your heart, the voice you've learned to ignore in the midst of ministry. Our goal is not to shame you or manipulate you into praying. No, we trust that God's Spirit through his word will do the necessary work of convicting you and increasing your desire to pray.

Introduction

We hope to accomplish this by highlighting a theme that occurs throughout Scripture. You are uniquely called by God to come before God on behalf of your people, pleading with God to work and move among your people. Simply stated, you have a calling to intercede for your flock. And our calling to intercede for our people follows the example of our Lord Jesus Christ and is made possible by his glorious intercession.

In the pages that follow, we'll look at how the work of prayer is a consistent biblical pattern for God's leaders (part 1). In the second half of the book, we'll highlight some of the practical aspects of praying that we hope will better equip you to pray for your flock. These are tools to help bring much-needed discipline to your life and ministry, restoring prayer to its proper place.

To better serve you and to make up for my deficiencies in prayer, I have asked my dear friend Ryan Fullerton to be my writing companion in this work. I understand what the Bible teaches and what God expects of us as praying pastors, but Ryan has modeled this for many years. I have developed some helpful systems and processes so I can effectively shepherd and pray for my church, but Ryan has a genuine passion to pray—a passion I often lack. Ryan has not only been a faithful pastor to his flock for over a decade; he has singlehandedly challenged me more than anyone in my life to be a more fervent pray-er for my own soul and the souls under my care.

Our prayer is that God will use this short book to inspire and motivate all shepherds of the Lord Jesus to be more fervent and faithful intercessors on behalf of God's people. We hope the motivation comes as they realize that Jesus is pleading before his Father on our behalf. Jesus is our advocate as we pray for our people. And our work is based on his intercession for us. May these glorious truths about our Mediator turn up the volume on the voice of our conscience and lead us to fervent, faithful prayer.

PART 1

WHAT DOES THE BIBLE TEACH?

Ryan Fullerton

CHAPTER 1

A CALL TO PRAYER

IF YOU'RE READING this book, you likely have a desire to pray for your people. Sadly, desire is rarely enough. When our Lord Jesus Christ asked his faithful inner circle of disciples to "stay here and keep watch with me" (Matthew 26:38), I'm sure they had a desire to stay with him and to support with their prayers the One they loved. Unfortunately, that desire was not enough. Instead, they became a memorable illustration of a painful truth that every pastor has experienced when it comes to prayer: "The spirit is willing, but the flesh is weak" (26:41). How many times have you made a fresh resolve to pray for your people only to find yourself fast asleep because your "eyes were heavy" (26:43)?

The goal of this book is to cultivate a passion for prayer in every pastor's heart. Every pastor needs to resonate with the focus of the New Testament apostles: "[We] will give our attention to prayer" (Acts 6:4). Specifically, we want to encourage you to pray for the people God has placed under your care as their shepherd and pastor. In the following chapters, we will paint a picture of how God's promises fuel our prayers, how we can fight to grow in prayer, and how we can plan to pray for our people proactively through the many different opportunities God gives us to intercede for them. But before we take any action, we need to be willing to confront our idols of busyness and sleepiness and commit to the great work of prayer. We must arm ourselves with a biblical understanding that will draw us into prayer.

It's my hope that this chapter will remind you that it is God who calls you to pray and that this high and holy calling should be among your top priorities as a pastor. With this in mind, I want to arm you with six biblical truths that can lead you to make prayer a priority.

1. Not praying for your people is a sin. Prayerlessness is sin. We need to be honest about this. A pastor who fails to pray for his people is as unbiblical as a pastor who refuses to preach God's word. One of the sweetest realities of being a Christian is that we're now "slaves to righteousness" (Romans 6:18). Despite "the desires of the flesh" pulling us toward sin (Galatians 5:16), believers have an insatiable desire to do what is right. Because God has written his law on our minds and in our hearts (Jeremiah 31:33; Hebrews 8:10), we desire to love righteousness and hate wickedness (Psalm 45:7; Hebrews 1:9). The Spirit never permits Christians to tolerate sin in their lives. Like the congregants they serve, pastors can never be happy tolerating prayerlessness in their lives, because prayerlessness is sin.

The prophet Samuel made this abundantly clear when he promised the people of Israel that he'd pray for them: "As for me, far be it from me that I should sin against the LORD by failing to pray for you" (1 Samuel 12:23). Samuel recognized that a failure to pray for God's people was a sin against God. Samuel was a leader among God's people. How could he claim to care for them when he didn't bring their needs before Yahweh-Yireh (Genesis 22:14), the One who alone could care for those needs? And how could Samuel claim to lead God's people if he didn't lead them to seek the Lord in prayer? To leave God's people unprayed for is to leave them uncared for, unprovided for, and unled — "like sheep without a shepherd" (Matthew 9:36). As pastors, we're called to flee sin and to pursue righteousness. We must learn to flee the sin of prayerlessness and to put on the righteous and wonderful habit of praying for our people.

2. Praying for your people glorifies God. One of my favorite verses in the Bible on prayer is Psalm 50:15 (ESV): "Call upon me in the day of trouble; I will deliver you, and you shall glorify me." One of my ministerial mentors used to say, "The Christian life is full of trouble. You are either just coming out of trouble, in the midst of trouble, or on your way into trouble." Indeed, the Christian life is not supposed to be easy. Jesus promised that in this life we will have trouble (John 16:33) — and this is even more certain when we are called to lead God's people. And yet every day of trouble is a day we have the opportunity and privilege of glorifying God. In comforting the sick, discipling new converts, and counseling people in difficult situations, we can sometimes feel like we are being distracted from our true calling, but to think this way is a mistake. Each and every trouble that comes our way is an opportunity to honor God as we call on him for help — and he helps us! When he answers our prayers and works in the lives of the people we're praying for, he gets the glory. When he comforts the sick or fixes the logistical issues we've been having, he gets the glory because he did the work. Follow the advice of John Newton (1725 – 1807), who wrote these words in one of his hymns:

> Come, my soul, thy suit prepare,
> Jesus loves to answer prayer;
> He himself has bid thee pray,
> Therefore will not say thee nay;
> Therefore will not say thee nay.
>
> Thou art coming to a King,
> Large petitions with thee bring;
> For his grace and pow'r are such,
> None can ever ask too much;
> None can ever ask too much.[1]

If we ask the Lord to work in the midst of our troubles, we'll give him the glory he deserves.

3. *We are called to imitate leaders who pray for their people.* Hebrews 13:7 urges us to think about the great leaders in the church: "Remember your leaders, who spoke the word of God to you. Consider the outcome of their way of life and imitate their faith." If you survey the great leaders of the Christian church, one thing they have in common is this: they were committed to prayer. We see this in the life of the apostle Paul, who told the Colossians that he and his partners in the ministry "have not stopped praying" for them since the day he heard about them (Colossians 1:9). What an example of

perseverance! Nonstop prayer since the first day he knew about the Colossian sheep. Consider that, brothers, and imitate this way of life. Consider also the example of Epaphras, "who is one of you and a servant of Christ Jesus," and the one Paul tells us was "always wrestling in prayer for you, that you may stand firm in all the will of God, mature and fully assured" (Colossians 4:12). Remember the example of godly men like Paul and Epaphras; they were men of prayer.

4. *Praying for your people reflects the priority of the early church.* Pentecost, the outpouring of the Holy Spirit on God's people, was an answer to prayer. The earliest Christian leaders, along with slightly more than a hundred followers of Christ, were praying and waiting when God suddenly moved in power (Acts 1 – 2). The earliest Christians "devoted themselves ... to prayer" (Acts 2:42), and as the church grew and the demands of leadership increased, the leaders realized they needed to reset their priorities. The neglect of some of the widows had helped them realize they couldn't do everything. But what *should* their focus be? Should they focus on benevolence or administration? These were good and spiritual options (Romans 12:6 – 8), but the leaders of the early church knew that one thing was best. Under the leadership of the Holy Spirit, they proclaimed, "It would not be right for us to neglect the ministry of the word of God in order to wait on tables. Brothers and sisters, choose seven men from among you who are known to be full of the Spirit and wisdom. We will turn this responsibility over to them and will give our attention to prayer and the ministry of the word" (Acts 6:2 – 4).

Did you notice what made the cut? For the leaders of the

church of God there could be no neglecting of prayer and the study and teaching of the Scriptures. The corporate church couldn't leave the widows to starve, of course. But the leaders realized they would lose everything if they gave up on prayer. All the generosity required to care for the widows would have dried up if the leaders hadn't continued to dip their buckets into the well of God's mercy through prayer for God's people. If we want to have New Testament ministries, then we must understand and practice the New Testament priority given to prayer.

5. *Praying for God's people will lead them to change.* As pastors, we long to see our people growing and changing. This is one of the reasons we do what we do. We long to see the Lord Jesus Christ make his people more Christlike by the power of the Holy Spirit. Because we long for this, we do what we think will help our people grow. We prepare sermons because we believe in the life-changing power of the Bible. We set an example for the flock because we know people follow their leaders. But do we pray? Do we believe that the power of God on our efforts is unleashed through prayer? To be clear, we need counseling, preaching, and training opportunities. But we must confess that all of these are useless without the power of God unleashed through prayer. The apostle Paul saw prayer as one of the primary means of promoting the sanctification of God's people. That is why he prayed:

> We continually ask God to fill you with the knowledge of his will through all the wisdom and understanding that the Spirit gives, so that you may live a life worthy

of the Lord and please him in every way: bearing fruit in every good work, growing in the knowledge of God, being strengthened with all power according to his glorious might so that you may have great endurance and patience.

Colossians 1:9 – 11

Knowledge, wisdom, understanding, life change, fruit bearing, strength, power, endurance, patience — for the apostle Paul, all of these came to God's people through prayer.

In his letter to the Philippians, Paul writes, "And this is my prayer: that your love may abound more and more in knowledge and depth of insight, so that you may be able to discern what is best and may be pure and blameless for the day of Christ, filled with the fruit of righteousness that comes through Jesus Christ — to the glory and praise of God" (Philippians 1:9 – 11).

Love, knowledge, depth of insight, discernment, purity, blamelessness, the fruit of righteousness to the praise and glory of God — here we see again that all of these blessings came through prayer. Do the congregations we serve manifest these characteristics? Perhaps they don't because we "do not ask God" (James 4:2). Oh, Lord, move us to pray!

6. *Prayer is how ordinary men do extraordinary things for God.* For years, the elders at the church I serve have sought to be obedient to God's call to pray for the sick in accordance with James 5:14. Each time we gather with one of God's suffering saints to ask the Lord to heal them, I'm encouraged by a single verse in the book of James. James reminds us that "Elijah was a human being, even as we are. He prayed earnestly that it would not rain, and it did not rain on the land for three and

a half years" (5:17). I've always felt that it is a tender mercy of God to place this verse near the end of chapter 5.

Think about this. James has just told the sick to call the church elders to pray over a sick person in the hope they will be healed. James seems to think healing won't come once in a blue moon, but that it is something we should expect God to do. He writes, "The prayer offered in faith will make the sick person well; the Lord will raise them up" (5:15). What a promise! The elders are asking God to do a miracle. James knows how the average pastor is going to think: "Who, *me*? I'm just an ordinary man!" James anticipates this objection and writes, "Elijah was a man with a nature like ours, and he prayed fervently that it might not rain, and for three years and six months it did not rain on the earth. Then he prayed again, and heaven gave rain, and the earth bore its fruit" (5:17 – 18 ESV).

James is saying, "Look, elders, you're just like Elijah, the one whom God used to change the weather patterns for three and a half years. Surely God can use an average man like you to do extraordinary things." What an encouragement! We don't need to be extraordinary for God to do extraordinary things through our ministry. Instead, we should fully and joyfully embrace our ordinariness and grab hold of the extraordinary promises of God.

Brothers, it is my hope that these six truths will shape your conscience and move your heart toward deeper passion and resolve to pray. Give yourself over to prayer for your people. Our obedience flows out of minds that are transformed by God's word (Romans 12:1 – 2). So let your renewed mind lead you to a fresh resolve to pray. Prayer gives glory to God, follows the example of great men of the past, reflects the priority of the early church, changes our people, and is used by God to allow ordinary men to do extraordinary things. May God help us to pray!

CHAPTER 2

UNDERSTANDING INTERCESSION
Brian Croft

THE BIBLE IS an amazing story, a fact we sometimes forget. It tells us the story of our Creator, the Lord and sustainer of the universe, who is working to redeem his rebellious creation. By understanding the story of the Bible, we better understand how God works in history and consequently obtain a better grasp of who he is and what he is saying to us.

In the biblical narrative, we see that God created a pristine world; it was good and perfect (Genesis 1–2). We learn that Adam and Eve rebelled against God (Genesis 3), corrupting God's creation by introducing sin into the world. One consequence was relational separation between God and those he created in his image. Yet all was not lost, for God had a plan to reconcile his creation from this separation and renew his marred image in his image bearers. One of the ways God implements this is by appointing leaders who love and care for his people in many ways, including pleading with God for the needs and concerns of the people. The word that best describes this particular role of godly leaders is *intercession*.

Abraham, the Intercessor on Behalf of Sodom

God determined that his chosen nation would come through Abraham, and, as a result, all the nations of the earth would be blessed (Genesis 18:18). God chose Abraham for a specific purpose: "so that he will direct his children and his household after him to keep the way of the LORD by doing what is right and just, so that the LORD will bring about for Abraham what he has promised him" (18:19).

Immediately following these words, God demonstrates his righteousness and justice by declaring judgment to come on Sodom and Gomorrah for the grievousness of their sin (Genesis 18:20). As God reveals his intent to judge the wicked in Sodom and Gomorrah, Abraham pleads to God on behalf of any righteous who may exist in the city:

> The men turned away and went toward Sodom, but Abraham remained standing before the LORD. Then Abraham approached him and said: "Will you sweep away the righteous with the wicked? What if there are fifty righteous people in the city? Will you really sweep it away and not spare the place for the sake of the fifty righteous people in it? Far be it from you to do such a thing—to kill the righteous with the wicked, treating the righteous and the wicked alike. Far be it from you! Will not the Judge of all the earth do right?"
> The LORD said, "If I find fifty righteous people in the city of Sodom, I will spare the whole place for their sake."
>
> Genesis 18:22 – 26

Pray for the Flock

What continues through the end of the chapter is this dialogue between God and his chosen servant, who appeals to God to spare the city if just a few righteous are found. God answers Abraham's appeal; and though the wicked city was still destroyed, Abraham's prayer saved the few righteous who remained, including Lot (Genesis 19:19). Abraham establishes before his descendants are even born that God appoints leaders to whom, when they intercede on behalf of others, God listens.

Moses, the Intercessor on Behalf of Israel

As the story of God's redemption continues, God's promise of a great nation to come from Abram's offspring is fulfilled (Genesis 15). In God's appointed time, the future generations of Abraham's offspring multiplied and formed a great nation — Israel. And one of the most significant leaders of Israel was a man named Moses. Moses was appointed by God to lead his people and to play a mediating role between Israel and God. Moses regularly spoke to God on behalf of the people, bringing their needs and concerns before the Lord. His intercessory role is seen when he led the people out of the bondage of Egypt. And then, as they made their way through the wilderness, the Israelites made a golden calf and committed idolatry against the Lord, inciting God's anger:

> Then the Lord said to Moses, "Go down [from Mount Sinai], because your people, whom you brought up out of Egypt, have become corrupt. They have been quick to turn away from what I commanded them and have made themselves an idol cast in the shape of a calf.

They have bowed down to it and sacrificed to it and have said, 'These are your gods, Israel, who brought you up out of Egypt.'"

"I have seen these people," the LORD said to Moses, "and they are a stiff-necked people. Now leave me alone so that my anger may burn against them and that I may destroy them. Then I will make you into a great nation."

But Moses sought the favor of the LORD his God. "LORD," he said, "why should your anger burn against your people, whom you brought out of Egypt with great power and a mighty hand? Why should the Egyptians say, 'It was with evil intent that he brought them out, to kill them in the mountains and to wipe them off the face of the earth'? Turn from your fierce anger; relent and do not bring disaster on your people. Remember your servants Abraham, Isaac and Israel, to whom you swore by your own self: 'I will make your descendants as numerous as the stars in the sky and I will give your descendants all this land I promised them, and it will be their inheritance forever.'" Then the LORD relented and did not bring on his people the disaster he had threatened.

Exodus 32:7 – 14

God had just miraculously delivered his people and how did they show their gratitude? By committing idolatry. Is it any wonder that the Lord's anger burned against them and that God was ready to destroy the Israelites (Exodus 32:10)? And yet he doesn't. Why? Because Moses, the leader of God's people, intercedes on their behalf. He passionately cries out to the Lord, pleading with him to show mercy (32:11 – 13). He reminds the Lord of his promises to Abraham, Isaac, and Jacob. It is the honor of God's name that is at stake. As a result of the earnest pleas of Moses, the Lord relents and does not destroy his people (32:14). Moses intercedes, and the Lord shows mercy.

Moses was not a perfect leader, nor was he a perfect intercessor. Israel would continue in a long-standing pattern of disobedience to the Lord for generations. Yet even in the Israelites' failures, sins, and disobedience, the Lord remained faithful to his covenant.

King David, the Intercessor

Over time, the people pleaded for a king to rule them, and the Lord eventually gave them King David. David was not just God's appointed king; he was the recipient of another covenant promise, namely, that one of David's sons would rule forever over God's kingdom, an everlasting kingdom that will never pass away (2 Samuel 7:12–16). Even though David was an imperfect king who sinned grievously against the Lord (2 Samuel 11–12), he demonstrated faithfulness to rule over God's people and pleaded for the Lord's blessing, presence, and care on them. The psalms are filled with examples of King David going before the Lord as the people's advocate to praise God for his goodness to them, pleading for his forgiveness of their disobedience, and asking for the Lord's protection against their enemies. Psalm 28 is a great example of this:

> The LORD is my strength and my shield;
>> my heart trusts in him, and he helps me.
> My heart leaps for joy,
>> and with my song I praise him.

Understanding Intercession

The LORD is the strength of his people,
  a fortress of salvation for his anointed one.
Save your people and bless your inheritance;
  be their shepherd and carry them forever.

Psalm 28:7 – 9, emphasis added

David was not a perfect king, yet he trusted in the Lord. David knew his God was sovereign over all his enemies. David relied on the Lord for strength for himself and for his people. David knew the Lord would save them and would be the shepherd of his people. Because of this, David cries out to the Lord for help, asking the Lord on behalf of his people to save and rescue them. David praises the Lord on behalf of the people.

Jesus, Our Intercessor

Though David models for us much of what God's king is to be and represent, all of the imperfect, God-appointed leaders of Israel who followed were a shadow of the perfect mediator to come who would reconcile God's people to himself. Jesus Christ came as the Son of David foretold in the Old Testament (2 Samuel 7:12 – 16). As the Son of David (Matthew 1:1; Luke 1:32), Jesus was more faithful than David and better than Moses (Hebrews 3:3). Jesus did what no other leader of God's people could do, namely, give his sinless life for the sins of the people. In doing this, he not only became the perfect mediator of his people; he reconciled us to God. The Bible tells us that Jesus is now the great and perfect high priest foreshadowed in the old covenant sacrifices. He is the high priest of a better covenant, one with better promises (Hebrews 8:6). The most vivid picture of this, Jesus as the intercessor of his people, is found in a passage from the gospel of John known as the "high priestly prayer." Here Jesus prays for his disciples just before going to the cross:

> I pray for them. I am not praying for the world, but for those you have given me, for they are yours. All I have is yours, and all you have is mine. And glory has come to me through them. I will remain in the world no longer, but they are still in the world, and I am coming to you. *Holy Father, protect them by the power of your name*, the name you gave me, so that they may be one as we are one … My prayer is not that you take them out of the world but that *you protect them from the evil one*. They are not of the world, even as I am not of it. *Sanctify them by the truth*; your word is truth. As you sent me into the world, I have sent them into the world. For them I sanctify myself, that they too may be truly sanctified.
>
> John 17:9 – 11, 15 – 19, emphasis added

This prayer reveals the eternal relationship Jesus, the Son of God, has with his Father. Jesus appeals to his Father on behalf of his disciples, asking for their protection. Jesus asks the Father to keep them from the evil one and sanctify them in the truth.

Unlike the intercessors of the Old Testament, Jesus comes before the Father as an equal, and his requests on behalf of the people are based on who he is and what he has done. His death on the cross and resurrection from the grave purchased his people and redeemed them from the penalties of sin. Jesus does more than deliver a message to the people; his work provides unhindered, eternal access to the Father. The author of the letter to the Hebrews explains it this way:

> But when Christ came as high priest of the good things that are now already here, he went through the greater and more perfect tabernacle that is not made with human hands, that is to say, is not a part of this creation. He did not enter by means of the blood of goats and calves; but he entered the Most Holy Place once for all by his own blood, thus obtaining eternal redemption. The blood of goats and bulls and the ashes of a heifer sprinkled on those who are ceremonially unclean sanctify them so that they are outwardly clean. How much more, then, will the blood of Christ, who through the eternal Spirit offered himself unblemished to God, cleanse our consciences from acts that lead to death, so that we may serve the living God!
>
> For this reason Christ is the mediator of a new covenant, that those who are called may receive the promised eternal inheritance—now that he has died as a ransom to set them free from the sins committed under the first covenant.
>
> Hebrews 9:11–15

Because Jesus has now sealed the redemption of every single follower the Father has given him (John 17:6), followers of Jesus can come to the Father with a bold confidence, no longer separated from our Creator:

> Therefore, brothers and sisters, since we have confidence to enter the Most Holy Place by the blood of Jesus, by a new and living way opened for us through the curtain, that is, his body, and since we have a great priest over the

house of God, let us draw near to God with a sincere heart and with the full assurance that faith brings, having our hearts sprinkled to cleanse us from a guilty conscience and having our bodies washed with pure water.

Hebrews 10:19 – 22

Jesus appeals to the Father on behalf of his followers, and they are fully accepted as sons. Jesus purchased for his followers right standing with his Father, a standing that only he is worthy to hold. Yet he freely shares his access with us. God's redemptive plan to reconcile his people is effective through the sacrifice of Jesus (Hebrews 10:14). As a result, sinners and rebels against God are now adopted as sons of God. These blood-bought believers in Jesus Christ are united by Christ in faith and are indwelt by the Holy Spirit. They have become his body — the church.

The Apostles, Intercessors for the Church

Since Jesus has brought full reconciliation between God and his redeemed people, the church is able to appeal to God on its own through the mediating work of Jesus Christ, who now always lives to make intercession for them (Hebrews 7:25). As the apostles establish the early church, leaders emerge who shepherd God's people on behalf of the Chief Shepherd (1 Peter 5:4). The apostles modeled for other leaders a ministry of prayer (Acts 6:4) and then defined this role in their instructions to the different churches. Paul gives instructions, makes appeals to God on behalf of the church, and through Christ's mediating work models the pattern of God's appointed leaders appealing to God and interceding on behalf of the church:

Understanding Intercession

> And pray in the Spirit on all occasions with all kinds of prayers and requests. With this in mind, be alert and always keep on praying for all the Lord's people. Pray also for me, that whenever I speak, words may be given me so that I will fearlessly make known the mystery of the gospel, for which I am an ambassador in chains. Pray that I may declare it fearlessly, as I should.
>
> Ephesians 6:18–20

Paul writes to the church in Ephesus and asks them to pray. He says they should pray *always* and on *all* occasions. They should pray, specifically, for the Lord's people. They should pray for Paul and his work of proclaiming the gospel. Paul wrote these words, knowing there were faithful pastors (elders) in place (Acts 20:17–38) who would model for their Ephesian flock how to pray (1 Peter 5:3).

James also embraced the intercessory role of elders and leaders, calling them to pray on behalf of their people:

> Is anyone among you in trouble? Let them pray. Is anyone happy? Let them sing songs of praise. Is anyone among you sick? Let them call the elders of the church to pray over them and anoint them with oil in the name of the Lord. And the prayer offered in faith will make the sick person well; the Lord will raise them up. If they have sinned, they will be forgiven. Therefore confess your sins to each other and pray for each other so that you may be healed. The prayer of a righteous person is powerful and effective.
>
> James 5:13 – 16

James exhorts believers to call on their appointed shepherds to pray with them and for them, indicating that even though all believers now have access to the Father through Jesus Christ, there is still a need for Christian leaders to intercede on behalf of their people. The New Testament calls on Christians to look to their leaders for prayer and urges that prayer be seen as central to congregational life.

Pastors, Intercessors for Their People

This is a brief overview of the work of intercession, but what we learn is that God's redemptive plan and pattern have led to the establishment of the church, where those from every nation, tribe, people, and language are transformed through the gospel of Jesus Christ. As redeemed people are brought into a local church, those who shepherd on behalf of the Chief Shepherd (1 Peter 5:1–4) and care for the souls of Christ's redeemed people (Hebrews 13:17) are also called to pray for each soul entrusted to their care. Praying with people and pleading on their behalf before the Father are essential aspects of shepherding God's people. Pastors must pray. Elders must plead before God on behalf of their people. Leaders must lift to the throne of grace the needs of the church, both the church's needs as a whole and the needs of individual believers. The ministry of prayer enables the ministry of God's Spirit and equips the whole body of Christ to obey the commands of Scripture.

From the beginning, this pattern of intercession has been a part of God's design to redeem his people. God appoints leaders to serve as intercessors, representing the needs of the people to God. Today, through the work of Christ, every believer now has full access to the throne of God. This does not mean the prayers of a pastor are somehow better or more effective; yet, as we see in the New Testament church, pastors still have a special responsibility to diligently appeal for their people. Their calling is not one of privileged access; it is one of loving responsibility. And it is all of grace.

In the following chapters, we will dive a bit deeper into additional Scriptures to flesh out a biblical understanding of prayer. As we do, let us not lose sight of the compelling story of a good and sovereign God who is redeeming his rebellious people through the intercession of chosen leaders and eventually by means of our perfect and sufficient intercessor—Jesus Christ.

CHAPTER 3

PRAYER AND THE WORD

AS WE SAID in chapter 1, every pastor who has been called by God senses a God-given desire to pray. Yet many of us struggle to turn these desires into action. Too often, we sluggishly fail to make prayer a priority. Even though the Spirit cultivates in us holy desires for prayer, these desires are opposed by our flesh, by our own selfish and sinful desires: "For the flesh desires what is contrary to the Spirit" (Galatians 5:17). As a result, we often resemble the disciples James, John, and Peter, who were found sleeping instead of watching and praying (Matthew 26:36–46).

Sadly, when we consistently fail to pursue our God-given desires to pray, the desires wane, and our efforts at ministry become flaccid and weak. The prayer meetings we lead reflect the sleepiness of our own souls. Instead of growing in our faith and our desire for the Lord, we inspire naps. Instead of developing warriors who struggle "not against flesh and blood, but against the rulers, against the authorities, against the powers of this dark world and against the spiritual forces of evil in the heavenly realms" (Ephesians 6:12), we communicate that prayer does not matter all that much. If we want to live lives worthy of our calling (4:1), if we want to follow Christ, our "pioneer [captain/leader]" (Hebrews 2:10), then we must find the motivation to passionately ask, seek, and knock (Matthew 7:7 – 8) at the open door of the living God.

So what can motivate a pastor to pray? What will lift our souls to see the Lord with fresh eyes, lifting us out of the dangers of spiritual lethargy and awakening us to the passion, fellowship, and urgency of true intercessory prayer?

There are many voices calling for our attention. There is a family to care for, a sermon to study for, shut-ins to visit, meetings to attend, events to plan, emails to answer, phone calls to return, neighbors to evangelize, staff and volunteers to mobilize. And there are those never-ending fires we must continually put out. But we need to focus our attention on the voice of the Lord as he calls us into the secret place to be with him. And the only voice capable of gripping our attention and moving us to our knees is the word of God. It "is alive and active" and "sharper than any double-edged sword" (Hebrews 4:12).

For the pastor who is lacking in desire to pray, I recommend turning to the word of God and listening to the Lord speak through his written word.

The Example of Daniel

In Daniel 9, we find a powerful example of a Christlike man motivated by God's word to pray for God's people:

Pray for the Flock

In the first year of Darius son of Xerxes (a Mede by descent), who was made ruler over the Babylonian kingdom—in the first year of his reign, I, Daniel, understood from the Scriptures, according to the word of the LORD given to Jeremiah the prophet, that the desolation of Jerusalem would last seventy years. So I turned to the Lord God and pleaded with him in prayer and petition, in fasting, and in sackcloth and ashes.

Daniel 9:1–3

When Daniel was in his early teens, his life was utterly uprooted. In 605 BC, King Nebuchadnezzar of Babylon besieged Israel's capital city and looted it. He took all of the city's finest treasures and their sacred vessels, and he captured the best and brightest of Jerusalem's future generation, taking them on a six-hundred-mile forced march to the capital of his kingdom. One of the young Hebrew men on that march was Daniel, a man "without any physical defect, handsome, showing aptitude for every kind of learning, well informed, quick to understand, and qualified to serve in the king's palace" (Daniel 1:4).

Daniel was removed from his home, taken out of his comfort zone from the land he loved and made a captive in a foreign kingdom. Yet despite living in exile, Daniel never forgot where he was from. Although he lived in Babylon for decades and saw multiple kings and kingdoms come and go, his internal clock still beat on Jerusalem's time zone. When God answered Daniel's lengthy prayer (Daniel 9:4–19), Daniel mentions that it happened "about the time of the evening sacrifice" (9:21). Even years after Daniel was forced to leave his beloved Jerusalem, living far from the temple, he still marked time by the temple that had been destroyed.

Year after year, the prophet lived in exile, far from the promised land he loved. Can you sense the homesick throbbing that gnawed at Daniel's soul? Imagine how Daniel must have felt the day he was studying the Bible and came across the promise that *his people would go home*. In Daniel 9, we see Daniel reading the Scriptures "according to the word of the LORD given to Jeremiah the prophet." In his reading, Daniel "understood" from the book of Jeremiah "that the desolation of Jerusalem would last *seventy years*" (Daniel 9:2, emphasis added). As Daniel read those prophetic words, he would have understood that his exile — and the exile of his people — was coming to a close.

Israel would be restored after seventy years of captivity. Daniel was likely reading what Jeremiah the prophet had written years earlier in Jeremiah 29:10 – 11: "This is what the LORD says: 'When seventy years are completed for Babylon, I will come to you and fulfill my good promise to bring you back to this place. For I know the plans I have for you,' declares the LORD, 'plans to prosper you and not to harm you, plans to give you hope and a future.'"

I can only imagine how Daniel's heart must have raced as he began to absorb the hope of God's word and understand the power of God's promises. Daniel knew from the word of God that his people would indeed be returned to the land he loved.

The Word Moved Daniel to Pray

How did Daniel respond? The word of God motivated Daniel
to pray. Notice that when Daniel discovered this promise, he
did not immediately start walking back to Jerusalem. He did
not start a political organization to advocate for the freedom
of Israel. He did not petition the king for the freedom of the
Jews. He simply prayed.

Daniel knew from his reading that God would do what
he had said he would do. The authority and the certainty of
the word of God brought Daniel to his knees. And the same
is true for us today. God's word leads us to prayer, and prayer
leads us to God's word. As pastors, we grow weary as we wait
to see lives transformed. We minister and wait. Our people
are spiritually a long way from where we want them to be,
but God's word promises that he will bring them along. God
promises that he "who began a good work in you will bring
it to completion at the day of Jesus Christ" (Philippians 1:6
ESV). Like Daniel, as we rediscover God's promises, it should
move us to pray that God will bring it to pass.

Here's an idea: as you study God's word, every time you
come across one of God's promises, stop and pray for a particular person in your congregation. Pray that God's promise
will be realized in their life. For example, think of a person
in your church whose sanctification seems slow or stalled. In
the new covenant, God promises, "I will put my Spirit in you
and move you to follow my decrees and be careful to keep my
laws" (Ezekiel 36:27). When you come across this promise,
stop and pray that our promise-keeping God will spiritually
move the people you care for into more careful obedience to

his commands. Don't just read God's promises. Like Daniel, pray them. Ask God to bring them into reality!

When we know what God is going to do, it should produce confidence in us. And this confidence will provide the motivation to pray. As believers, we already want the things the word of God promises because the Holy Spirit is dwelling in us (1 Corinthians 3:16). The new life of "Christ in [us], the hope of glory" (Colossians 1:27) causes us to love God and to love the brethren. And the promises of God in his word tell us he is going to glorify his name and empower and grow our brothers and sisters in the faith. God's promises are the sweet assurances that he will do what our hearts long for him to do.

The Way God Works

At this point, some may be wondering, *If God has promised he will do something, then why bother praying? Why ask for something if God has already said he will give it?* We've all wrestled with this question. And it's a question that honors God because it recognizes that he is sovereign and faithful and does not need our prayers to accomplish his will. At the same time, we need to guide our practice not by our own reasoning but by God's revelation.

The answer we find in the Bible is that God is a God who promises *what* he will do, but he is also a God who promises *how* he will do it. God ordains the *ends* and the *means*. He promises us a certain destination, yet he also decides how we will reach that destination. And in this case, God has decided he is most glorified in accomplishing his purposes by answering the prayers of his people. We see this principle at work in the original promise God makes in Jeremiah 29. Right after seeing God's promise that he will—beyond a doubt—bring Israel back to the promised land, Daniel would have read this:

> "Then you will call on me and come and pray to me, and I will listen to you. You will seek me and find me when you seek me with all your heart. I will be found by you," declares the LORD, "and will bring you back from captivity. I will gather you from all the nations and places where I have banished you," declares the LORD, "and will bring you back to the place from which I carried you into exile."
>
> Jeremiah 29:12–14

God's promise to bring his people back from exile includes the declaration that he will accomplish their return *through the prayers of his exiled people*. Daniel knew this, and so he prayed. And he didn't pray halfheartedly; he prayed with his whole heart. He prayed repentantly with "pleas for mercy" (Daniel 9:3 ESV). He prayed intensely to God "in fasting, and in sackcloth and ashes" (9:3). He prayed confidently, crying out, "Lord, listen! Lord, forgive. Lord, hear and act! For your sake, my God, do not delay" (9:19). Daniel didn't just accept the promise that God would move his people. He saw that God's movement would come as a response to the prayers of his people.

Don't let your theological presuppositions negate the clear word that God has given. We need to understand that God is eager to move, and he has promised to move *through* our prayers. If we lack what God has promised, the reason may be that we have not asked God. The Scriptures say this clearly—even bluntly: "[We] do not have because [we] do not ask God" (James 4:2). God has promised to sanctify his people. He has also promised to sanctify them through our prayers. This truth should cause us to pray more frequently and fervently.

Motivated to Pray!

Our prayers, by the sovereign will of God, are essential to the advancement of his redemptive plan and purpose. And best of all, the results are guaranteed when we pray according to God's word, clinging to his promises. When we pray in accord with God's word, we advance the cause of Christ throughout the world. We witness his work of sanctification in the people we serve. Our heavenly Father has given us every reason to approach the task of prayer confidently and to do it with zeal. His word tells us *what* he is going to do and then calls us to *ask* him to do it.

Far from making prayer an afterthought, this realization should strengthen our desire to pray. The words of Wayne Grudem are helpful: "We should have great confidence that God will answer our prayer when we ask him for something that accords with a specific promise or command of Scripture like this [referring to James 1:5–8]. In such cases, we know what God's will is, because he has told us, and we simply need to pray believing that he will answer."[2]

My fellow pastors, know that Jesus has assured us that "whoever believes in me will do the works I have been doing, and they will do even greater things than these" (John 14:12). And to all of God's spiritually adopted children has been given the pledge that they will receive the power of the Holy Spirit. This third Person of the Trinity will empower us to be witnesses "to the ends of the earth" (Acts 1:8).

We know these things because God has promised that Christ's blood has "purchased for God persons from every tribe and language and people and nation" (Revelation 5:9). The promises of the Bible should lead us to pray. We should ask ourselves, Are the sheep the Lord has given me truly walking in the joy of Christ's presence? Are they overflowing with rivers of Spirit-empowered blessing for others? Are they advancing the sure mission of Christ into all the world? Are they doing greater things than the Lord did?

If not, before you do anything else, pray. Your people can do these things. Christ has promised them to us, and we now must ask. The results are guaranteed by the promises of God. His promises are the source and goal of our prayers.

CHAPTER 4

PRAYER AND FAITH

IN THE LAST chapter, we saw how the promises of the word of God can ignite our prayers. Yet sadly, many of us find the promises of God too hot to handle, a bit outside of our comfort zone. Take a few of them, for example:

> "Truly, I say to you, whoever says to this mountain, 'Be taken up and thrown into the sea,' and does not doubt in his heart, but believes that what he says will come to pass, it will be done for him. Therefore I tell you, whatever you ask in prayer, believe that you have received it, and it will be yours."
>
> Mark 11:23–24 ESV

> "Very truly I tell you, whoever believes in me will do the works I have been doing, and they will do even greater things than these, because I am going to the Father. And I will do whatever you ask in my name, so that the Father may be glorified in the Son. You may ask me for anything in my name, and I will do it."
>
> John 14:12–14

Pray for the Flock

"If you believe, you will receive whatever you ask for in prayer."

Matthew 21:22

Do these red-hot promises of God light up your prayer closet each day? Do they light a fire in your bones? Or do you find yourself discounting them, covering them up with a wet blanket of unbelief? The promises of God can be hard to believe. And if you struggle to take them seriously, you are not alone.

We all know that prayer is never just a mechanical process of believing and receiving. At the same time, the promises of God aren't theological puzzles waiting to be solved; they are torches meant to set our damp souls ablaze. They aren't the words of a wild-eyed faith healer; they are the words of the holy Son of God whose promises are true, whose words are life to our dead hearts.

Most of us don't have a theology of prayer that is capable of getting us out of bed in the morning, let alone powerful enough to move mountains. Our theology is big enough to move us to preach, lead meetings, and visit hospital rooms, but is it leaving us unmotivated to approach God in persistent and passionate prayer? We refrain from coming boldly before God and asking him to remove the obstacles of sin and disobedience that stand in the way of a powerful kingdom advance in our churches and communities. Instead, we trust our own activity rather than waiting on the Lord to act through prayer.

Nothing will ever change until our hearts are changed, until we are sufficiently motivated to *want* to pray. Nothing will change until we learn to listen to Jesus when he says, "Very truly I tell you, my Father will give you whatever you ask in my name" (John 16:23). We are not motivated to pray because our view of God is too small. We are praying for God to repair potholes when we need him to move mountains. We pray for God to help us meet our budget when we should be praying for God to unleash a tidal wave of generosity that will advance the kingdom further and faster. We pray for God to give leaders wisdom in their decision making, but we don't pray for God to give our leaders a vision that is bigger and grander than our capacities. We keep asking God to help us achieve manageable goals; we need to be asking God to relocate mountains!

Lying before us are countless obstacles blocking the advance of the gospel. There are discouraged saints, legalistic Bible study teachers, families whose loyalty to each other surpasses their loyalty to Christ, and financial and political hurdles. But Jesus can deal with all of that! I believe one of our great High Priest's deepest desires is to show his people that prayer can accomplish the impossible. Prayer is what we need, more than anything else, to advance the kingdom. And Jesus is eager to spur on our faith, using his word to fan the flickering flames of our feeble hopes and dreams.

Jesus Loves to Provoke the Faith of People of Faith

Mark 11 records a story telling us that God's people are a people of faith, and that Jesus loves to stir up our faith. It's a story that reminds pastors not to downplay the radical promises of God, but to stir up faith so it leads to greater prayer.

> As [Jesus and his disciples] passed by in the morning, they saw the fig tree withered away to its roots. And Peter

remembered and said to him, "Rabbi, look! The fig tree that you cursed has withered." And Jesus answered them, "Have faith in God. Truly, I say to you, whoever says to this mountain, 'Be taken up and thrown into the sea,' and does not doubt in his heart, but believes that what he says will come to pass, it will be done for him. Therefore I tell you, whatever you ask in prayer, believe that you have received it, and it will be yours. And whenever you stand praying, forgive, if you have anything against anyone, so that your Father also who is in heaven may forgive you your trespasses."

Mark 11:20–25 ESV

The passage begins with an awkward contrast. Peter innocently notices that the fig tree Jesus cursed the previous day has withered. He calls Jesus' attention to the tree: "Rabbi, look! The fig tree that you cursed has withered." Jesus gives a terse and somewhat awkward response: "Have faith in God." Peter says the cursed fig tree is withered; Jesus tells Peter he should have faith. What's going on here? Jesus' command sounds strange—until we remember the context.

The larger context (Mark 11:12–25) is structured much like a sandwich, a "meal" made up of three parts. We have the first slice of bread, then the meat in the middle, and then another slice of bread. In this passage before us, the first slice of bread is a curse. In verses 13–14, Jesus approaches a fruitless fig tree and curses it, saying, "May no one ever eat fruit from you again." Then we find the meat of the sandwich in verses 15–19. Jesus enters the temple and finds that the temple, *like the fig tree*, is fruitless as well. The temple is not as it should be — "a house of prayer for all the nations." Instead, the temple has become "a den of robbers" (verse 17). This fruitless religious institution arouses his holy anger. That's the meat of the story — the underlying conflict or problem. The final piece of bread is the passage cited above, verses 20 – 25. Here we see how Jesus responds to fruitless and prayerless religion. His curse leads it to wither and die. Peter reminds us that the tree has been cursed because of its fruitlessness. In verse 21, he says to Jesus, "Rabbi, look! The fig tree that you cursed has withered." The point is clear: if something does not produce fruit, it is cursed; it will wither and die.

Understanding the context of the story, we see this is a prophecy of what Jesus is going to do to the fruitless and prayerless religion of Israel. He is bringing it to an end. Once we understand the meaning of the cursed fig tree, we are better able to understand Jesus' response to Peter. Do you remember what he said? "Have faith in God." In the face of faithless religion, self-righteous prayer (Luke 18:9 – 14), legalistic pomp and circumstance (Matthew 6), and greedy, money-hungry leaders (Mark 11:15 – 19; cf. 1 Timothy 6:5), Jesus is calling Peter (and all God's people) to something different — a life not of empty religion but full of faith in God

We need to hear this word as well, just as Peter did nearly two thousand years ago. If you shepherd a flock, you will grow discouraged. You will struggle to believe that God is working. You will wrestle with doubts. So how do you respond? We must not shrink back in disbelief. We must cultivate a living, active, and prayerful faith in God.

Turning Up the Volume

But Jesus doesn't stop there. He calls Peter to faith and then excites and motivates him, whetting his appetite. Jesus goes on to provoke hunger in Peter's heart, inciting a desire to see God do the impossible. He says to Peter, "Truly, I say to you, whoever says to this mountain, 'Be taken up and thrown into the sea,' and does not doubt in his heart, but believes that what he says will come to pass, it will be done for him" (Mark 11:23 ESV).

Many people approach this verse with yellow caution lights flashing. Where Jesus would cultivate hunger and encourage us to embrace God-sized dreams, we give words of caution and urge restraint. Not that we should expect, based on this verse, that God will do whatever we want, whenever we want it. God is not someone we use to accomplish our purposes. Nor is this verse a blanket guarantee that God will move on our timeline. It's a Jewish figure of speech, and it means God is ready and willing to do the impossible. The point of this passage is not to say that faith is a force, that if you pray with enough desire and passion, you will be able to "name it and claim it." Instead, it is teaching that when we ask for the impossible to be done, and we ask in Jesus' name under his authority, we can ask with the confidence that we are heard and that God will respond.

Don't shine yellow lights into the hearts of your people and undermine the purpose of Jesus. He says these words so that our hearts might grow with faith-filled zeal. Jesus is giving us a green light here, challenging us to take God at his word.

Let me say this another way. If Christ's primary aim in this passage was to urge caution in our prayers, then he failed miserably. But if his aim was to spur men like John Knox (1514–1572) to pray, "Give me Scotland or I die," then *mission accomplished*. If Jesus intended to create men like George Müller (1805–1898), who would provide for orphans solely by faith in the provision of God, then he was successful. If his aim was to create churches that would pray their leaders out of jail (Acts 12) and raise servant-hearted women from the dead (9:36–43), then he accomplished it marvelously well.

This mountain-moving promise—and others like it—encourages us to believe that God can remove any obstacle (i.e., "mountain") in the way of advancing his kingdom. We read promises like these, and our vision of God is enlarged. We see him as he is—powerful and able to do whatever he wants. This gives us faith and motivation to come before him, asking him to overcome the obstacles that oppose his kingdom purposes.

It's true that God sometimes says no to our prayers (Deuteronomy 3:26; 2 Corinthians 12:8–9), and it's also true that we must not ask anything from the Lord for selfish desires (Mark 10:35–38; James 4:3). God sometimes says no. And he never promises to accommodate our sinful requests. But while these things are true, they aren't the thrust of Jesus' teaching here, are they? If we take Jesus at his word, it seems he believes there are times when it's good and right to lift the hearts and minds of God's people so they see God as willing, able, and committed to answering prayer.

Jesus stressed this over and over throughout his earthly ministry. In John 15:7, he said, "If you remain in me and my words remain in you, ask whatever you wish, and it will be done for you." Apparently, this teaching wasn't too dangerous to repeat, because he says it again in John 15:16: "You did not choose me, but I chose you and appointed you so that you might go and bear fruit—fruit that will last—and so that whatever you ask in my name the Father will give you." And in case we still didn't get the point, he repeats it a third time in John 16:23: "In that day you will no longer ask me anything. Very truly I tell you, my Father will give you whatever you ask in my name." When Jesus repeats a point three times in two chapters, we do well to pay attention. Notice that he isn't urging us to be cautious in our prayers; he is putting a defibrillator on our faith-less hearts, hoping to shock them into life again.

The wonderful promises of the Lord Jesus Christ were meant to lift our eyes to heaven and move us to trust God to move mountains—in our lives, in the church, and for the sake of kingdom advancement. Unlike the Israelites of old, who lived in continual unbelief (Romans 11:20, 23; Hebrews 3:19), God wants us to be people of mountain-moving faith. Without this kind of faith, our prayers will be weak and ineffective.

Making Mountain Movement Powerful

As I write this chapter I'm having a typical, average day. I'm dealing with a few mildly disappointing staff situations. One of our members is in the hospital with a child fighting cancer. We have a couple overseas seeking to find out if God is opening a door for them to serve. We have another couple ready to begin a cross-cultural mission assignment, but the mission agency will not send them. We're in the third year of a building campaign, and the building we wanted to purchase was just sold to another buyer. Our nursery will be overrun with children again this week. There are many obstacles and many blessings.

As I think about these things, I'm always tempted to share my concerns with my coworkers instead of praying. I'm tempted to skip prayer—talking to God—and start talking to the people around me. So what leads me to pray instead? It's the overwhelming conviction that God alone is the one who can truly help me. He may use the wisdom of my colaborers at times, but he alone can move mountains. He alone can do the impossible. When I remember this, I pray. I recall who God is and what he has said, and I'm compelled to pray.

Will you join me in praying right now? Let your heart be filled with hope as you allow yourself to see God as he really is, the Mountain Mover for whom nothing is impossible. By faith, look to God and his promises, remembering "we live by faith, not by sight" (2 Corinthians 5:7). And never forget that "without faith it is impossible to please God" (Hebrews 11:6). God delights in our childlike faith as we look to him in our deepest need, calling out for help when the way forward seems impossible. He is pleased to respond.

CHAPTER 5

PRAYER AND EXPERIENCE

PASTORS PREPARE SERMONS. They administer staff and train volunteers. They visit. They counsel. A good pastor seeks to love his people as best he can. Yet all of this work can be powerless and ineffective without prayer. If we fail to pray, none of our efforts will give the people we love and serve the very thing they need most.

And what is the great need of our flock? Their greatest need is to taste the sweetness of Christ in their souls. Maurice Roberts, a Free Church of Scotland pastor, insightfully wrote these words:

> Ecstasy and delight are essential to the believer's soul and they promote sanctification. We were not meant to live without spiritual exhilaration and the Christian who goes for a long time without the experience of heart-warming will soon find himself tempted to have his emotions satisfied from earthly things and not, as he ought, from the Spirit of God. The soul is so constituted that it craves

fulfillment from things outside itself and will embrace earthly joys for satisfaction when it cannot reach spiritual ones ... The believer is in spiritual danger if he allows himself to go for any length of time without tasting the love of Christ and savoring the felt comforts of a Savior's presence. *When Christ ceases to fill the heart with satisfaction, the soul of man will go in silent search of other lovers.*[3]

Do the lives of those in your church family show that they have tasted the sweetness of Christ? Or have they gone for quite some time without this "ecstasy and delight"? What about your own soul? Have you been overwhelmed by your work, by the demands of ministry? Have you lost heart? Have you personally experienced the sweet love of Christ lately?

If you haven't, you need a fresh taste of the power and presence of Christ. One of the most glorious prayers we find in the New Testament can guide us toward just that. We are encouraged to pray for and expect an ever-deepening experience of the love of Christ.

You Know You Want This!

Ephesians 3:14–21 is my favorite prayer in the Bible. What's not to love about it? In these eight verses, Paul prays for several realities that every Christian longs for and that every spiritual shepherd hopes to see in his sheep.

> For this reason I kneel before the Father, from whom every family in heaven and on earth derives its name. I pray that out of his glorious riches he may strengthen you with power through his Spirit in your inner being, so that

Christ may dwell in your hearts through faith. And I pray that you, being rooted and established in love, may have power, together with all the Lord's holy people, to grasp how wide and long and high and deep is the love of Christ, and to know this love that surpasses knowledge — that you may be filled to the measure of all the fullness of God.

Now to him who is able to do immeasurably more than all we ask or imagine, according to his power that is at work within us, to him be glory in the church and in Christ Jesus throughout all generations, for ever and ever! Amen.

Paul prays that each person in the church will be strengthened "with power through his Spirit in [their] inner being." He prays that we will know more of the reality of Christ dwelling in our hearts through faith. And is there anything more thrilling than seeing that saint who has been entangled in sin now enraptured with the breadth and length and height and depth of the love of Christ "that surpasses knowledge"? The nineteenth-century Scottish minister Thomas Chalmers famously described this experience of Christ's love as the "expulsive power of a new affection."[4] We taste God's love and affection for us, and it leads to a corresponding love for God, a love that roots out our desire for sin.

As we taste the fullness of Christ's love, it changes and transforms us. But to their shame, many pastors and leaders struggle with doubts in this area. As time passes, people fall back into sinful patterns, and we begin to question whether God's love truly has the power that God's word promises. Or we've seen so many people change so slowly that we've reduced our expectations of what God will do. We've become "realistic." In my observation, this is a pastoral euphemism for being weary, discouraged, unbelieving, and frustrated.

We want what Paul prays for here, but the problem is the people we're praying for. We think, *They're just not the "utterly overwhelmed by the love of God" type.* When we think like this, we're forgetting that God doesn't just save "types"—he is the Savior and Lord of all. Whoever they are, they are the type of people God wants to overwhelm with his character-changing love!

For What Reason?

You may have missed the beginning of this prayer. Notice that Paul starts with the phrase "for this reason" (Ephesians 3:14). He bows his knees before the Father "for this reason." What reason is he referring to? What moved Paul to ask God for a greater outpouring of his presence in the midst of his people? Seeing *why* Paul prayed can motivate us to pray for our people.

There are two options we should consider. The first is in the verse immediately preceding our text. Paul tells the Ephesians "not to be discouraged because of my sufferings for you, which are your glory" (Ephesians 3:13). In essence, he is saying, *I'm suffering, but don't let that get you down. It's for your good.* Then he goes into his prayer. If verse 13 is the reason for the prayer, Paul is saying that the Ephesian believers shouldn't be discouraged, and so he prays that they'll know more of God's presence and power to fight against this discouragement.

Of course, there's nothing wrong with this reason. When we are suffering for the good of others, it's good to pray for their spiritual power and awareness of God's love to increase. Yet something seems to be missing. Seeing Paul's suffering as the primary reason for this prayer feels like we're forcing a puzzle piece into a space where it doesn't quite fit.

I think there's another reason for Paul's prayer. It involves a bit of a rabbit trail — something every preacher should understand. So what's the reason? It's found *before* verse 1 of chapter 3 — at the end of chapter 2. And it's not Paul's suffering that motivates his prayer for the Ephesians; it's the amazing truth that Jewish Christians and Gentile (non-Jewish) Christians in Ephesus are now part of a single, living temple of God. This has been the point of chapter 2, where he specifically addresses Gentile Christians. Paul writes these words:

> Consequently, you are no longer foreigners and strangers, but fellow citizens with God's people and also members of his household, built on the foundation of the apostles and prophets, with Christ Jesus himself as the chief cornerstone. In him the whole building is joined together and rises to become a holy temple in the Lord. And in him you too are being built together to become a dwelling in which God lives by his Spirit.
>
> Ephesians 2:19–22

Do you see what Paul is saying here? He is telling these believers that they're part of God's household, that they are growing into a "temple" — a community in which God dwells by his Spirit. And that's an amazing blessing! God's people are the place where God dwells. This is the reason that moves Paul to pray.

Prayer and Experience

Now, in case you think this is just a trivial connection, I want to explain why this matters. As a pastor, I've learned that one of the things keeping us from praying with faith for our people is that we no longer see them as God sees them. Our sight is warped, twisted by our own frustration and disappointment. We see them according to their struggles, patterns, and sinful proclivities. If we allow these things to define our people, we'll never have much hope that they'll change. We'll certainly not have hope that they can be overwhelmed with the power and presence of God's love.

But if we see them as God's temple—as the people in whom God has chosen to take up residence—there is hope. Because temples were meant to be filled with glory.

So Much Glory They Couldn't Stand It!

There are two examples in the Old Testament when God fills his dwelling place with his glory. And both of these fillings happen as God takes his place in this new residence. The first occurs at the dedication of the tabernacle. We're told that "the glory of the LORD filled the tabernacle" (Exodus 40:35). Moses was not able to enter the tent of meeting because the cloud settled on it, and the glory of the Lord filled it.

The second time was just as wonderful as the first, if not more so. We're told that "the temple of the LORD was filled with the cloud, and the priests could not perform their service because of the cloud, for the glory of the LORD filled the temple of God" (2 Chronicles 5:13–14).

As amazing as these two incidents are, they pale in comparison to the glory that God has revealed in his living temple, the church of Jesus Christ. As followers of Jesus, we are now the temple of God, and God is building us "with power through his Spirit in [our] inner being" (Ephesians 3:16). He's doing this so that "Christ [and not merely a cloud] may dwell in [our] hearts through faith" (3:17). And he desires to overwhelm us with "the love of Christ ... that surpasses knowledge—that [we] may be filled to the measure of all the fullness of God" (3:18–19).

The message of Ephesians 3:14–21 is that our people are the very dwelling place of God, and God desires to build them up and fill them with unspeakable glory. He wants to overwhelm them with the breadth and length and height and depth of the love of Christ. He wants to meet with them so they will be filled with "all the fullness of God." When we pray, we aren't just praying our own desires for the people we serve; we are praying the will of God—that God will do what he loves to do, namely, dwell in his people and bring glory to his name.

What's Your Reason?

If you focus on the sins and shortcomings of your people, you will eventually grow discouraged. And you will probably stop praying. But when we look at what God has done and focus on what he wants to do, there is great reason to press on in prayer. Your church isn't just a collection of sinful, broken people. They are the building blocks of God's temple. They are still under construction, of course, but this is exactly where God wants to work. This is his plan and the focus of his attention and desire. And God wants your church to become experientially familiar with his presence and power. He wants your people to be overwhelmed by his love. Could it be that one of the reasons our people sink in their suffering and buckle so quickly when tempted to sin is that we've prayed so little for them to know the experiential sweetness of God's love?

Would our people be different if they knew more of the sweet love of God? D. A. Carson once shared the story of R. A. Torrey, who, "while he was reading the Scriptures and praying ... was so overwhelmed with a profound consciousness of God's love that he began to weep and weep. Eventually he asked God to show him no more: he could not bear it."[5] I trust you'll agree with me—we all need experiences like this to strengthen our faith and combat discouragement and doubt. Our people need them as well, and it's our glorious calling to pray this heavenly love down on them.

Today you may be seeing spiritual flatness in your people. Maybe every Sunday morning feels flat. Start right here, with Paul's prayer for the Ephesian church. It's just the thing to pray. It is, after all, not just a prayer for individuals; it's a prayer for the entire church. Paul prays that "together with all the Lord's holy people" they'd understand the breadth of God's love. God's love is a blessing that is most fully experienced in community.

I'm convinced one of the reasons ministry can be so discouraging is that we are strangers to the desires that motivate Paul's prayers in these verses. We're strangers to so much of what God wants us to experience through the Spirit. And while it is possible to overemphasize the experiential realities of our faith, I fear that too many of us do the opposite and underemphasize them. We need to go before the Lord and ask him for real power for our people and fresh manifestations of his loving presence.

These kinds of experiences aren't just stories we can read about, mere revivals of days gone by. They are meant to be the experiences of our churches *today*. Join me in praying this prayer, and then trust the Lord "to do immeasurably more than all we ask or imagine, according to his power that is at work within us, to him be glory in the church and in Christ Jesus throughout all generations, for ever and ever! Amen" (Ephesians 3:20–21).

CHAPTER 6

PRAYER AND OBSTACLES

AT THIS POINT, I hope you are convinced you need to pray. You will probably admit that prayer is important and necessary. You may even be eager to pray. But while desire is essential, and it is where we begin, desire alone does not always lead to action. Our good desires can be derailed by disobedience and distraction. The New Testament authors were well aware of this. They mention several obstacles that can keep us from acting on our good intentions. And even when we do pray, there are things that can keep us from praying with effectiveness. Our minds wander. We grow distracted. We forget what we want to pray for.

In this chapter, I want to examine three biblical obstacles to prayer, all of them drawn from the book of 1 Peter. My hope is that you can learn to dislodge these obstacles and overcome them so you will be empowered to pray more fruitfully for your people.

Disobedience

The first obstacle to effective prayer is really the first obstacle to every good thing in the Christian life: sin. In 1 Peter 3, the apostle gives instructions to husbands and wives: "Husbands, in the same way be considerate as you live with your wives, and treat them with respect as the weaker partner and as heirs with you of the gracious gift of life, so that nothing will hinder your prayers" (1 Peter 3:7).

Peter reminds husbands that God's commands have teeth. He calls husbands to live with their wives in an understanding way. Peter aims for the heart by reminding husbands of an important reason for loving their spouse: "so that nothing will hinder your prayers." I appreciate Eugene Peterson's paraphrase in *The Message*: "so your prayers don't run aground." How many men have bowed their heads and recited eloquent prayers, only to find their supplications to God have landed on deaf ears? Consider your own prayer life. Have your prayers "run aground"?

Obviously, God is not deaf. We know that an omniscient God hears every sound we make. But Peter tells us that our heavenly Father isn't moved to answer our requests when our relationships with others are broken. And this is especially true when it's a marriage relationship. Disobedience hinders our prayers. And for the unbeliever, this hindrance is nearly absolute. "If anyone turns a deaf ear to my instruction, even their prayers are detestable" (Proverbs 28:9).

For believers, however, there is still hope. Since God has impressed his law on our hearts, a true child of God won't be ignored by his heavenly Father. God listens to our prayers, but our sin can still hinder their efficacy. When our hearts are infected with worldly concerns and our prayers are motivated by a desire to "spend what [we] get on [our] pleasures" as James writes, we will "not receive" when we ask (James 4:3). When we're praying and then remember that our brother has something against us, we must leave what we are doing and make things right with him (Matthew 5:23–26). Sometimes the most significant thing you can do to improve your prayer life is to pick up the phone. You may need to call your wife to apologize. You may need to talk with a church member you've been avoiding. Repentance sweeps away the hindrance of sin.

This also means that having a healthy prayer life cannot be separated from the rest of your life. If you finish reading this book and begin to routinely pray through your church's membership directory, but you don't seek to "live at peace with everyone," to whatever extent you have control over it (Romans 12:18; cf. Hebrews 12:14), then your prayers will not hit the ground running. They will just hit the ground. Sometimes the most significant thing you can do to improve your prayer life and the spiritual life of your church isn't prayer. Could it be that you first need to get right with others before you will see revival in your church?

D. L. Moody had a powerful experience with this. The popular nineteenth-century evangelist told this story:

> I remember one town that Mr. [Ira] Sankey and I visited. For a week it seemed as if we were beating the air; there was no power in the meetings. At last, one day, I said that perhaps there was someone cultivating the unforgiving

spirit. The chairman of our committee, who was sitting next to me, got up and left the meeting right in view of the audience. The arrow had hit the mark, and gone home to the heart of the chairman of the committee. He had had trouble with someone for about six months. He at once hunted up this man and asked him to forgive him. He came to me with tears in his eyes, and said: "I thank God you ever came here." That night the inquiry room was thronged.[6]

God unleashes his blessings on us when we flee disobedience. Of course, none of us can be perfect this side of heaven. "If we claim to be without sin, we deceive ourselves and the truth is not in us" (1 John 1:8). But that doesn't mean God ignores our sin. We must still practice repentance, learning to cultivate a contrite spirit and to keep what older saints used to call "short accounts" with God. We can make sure we've asked the Lord daily to "forgive us our debts, as we also have forgiven our debtors" (Matthew 6:12) and to help us seek reconciliation in any broken relationship (Romans 12:18). If we want to pray with power for our people, we must flee disobedience and seek reconciliation.

Self-Control

Peter is remarkably practical and insightful when he writes later in this letter, "The end of all things is at hand; therefore be self-controlled and sober-minded for the sake of your prayers" (1 Peter 4:7 ESV). Peter tells us that because the end of the world is upon us, we should keep praying. We keep up a dialogue with our heavenly Father because we know this world is filled with trouble and suffering. We need the help that only prayer can provide, so Peter warns us of two additional obstacles to our prayer lives. The first is self-control.

At this point, I confess I'm glad my wife is not writing this book because she could easily use me as an illustration of how a lack of self-control hinders one's prayer life. I know all too well that going to bed late makes it difficult to wake up in the morning to pray. Continually checking our smartphones robs us of time we can devote to prayer. Eating too much makes us sleepy when we should be alert and engaged in prayer. The busyness of ministry swallows up the time we need to "give our attention to prayer and the ministry of the word" (Acts 6:4). Though my calling is to be set apart for the tasks of prayer and study of the word, I'm ashamed to say I've far too often been devoted to the word and to web surfing instead.

Brothers, if we are to pray for our people, we must set aside undistracted time to do this. We must clear our schedule and make time to pray each day. We must intentionally plan extended times to pray at different seasons in our lives and ministries. We must "cut off" our smartphones and "gouge out" our iPads (Matthew 5:29–30) so the constant buzzing of incoming emails, cell phone texts, app updates, Facebook statuses, and Twitter feeds don't destroy our own asking, seeking, and knocking (7:7).

As I write these words, I'm in the middle of an extended fast that is intended, in part, to help me conquer my bondage to food. While I'm not obese, my overeating has made me tired, sluggish, and, most importantly, useless in prayer. This is one way I'm seeking to be more effective in prayer.

What about you? What do you need to cut out or cut off

to make you more like Elijah the prophet, "a human being, even as we are," who "prayed earnestly" (James 5:17–18)? What would it look like for you to be truly devoted to prayer?

Presbyterian minister Floyd Doud Shafer has a wonderful illustration of what it looks like to prepare a man to be devoted to preaching. As you read this, apply what Shafer says about preaching to your own quest to make prayer a priority. Shafer emphasizes there are times when drastic measures must be taken to prepare a man to preach:

> Fling him into his office, tear the office sign from the door, and nail on the sign: *Study*. Take him off the mailing list, lock him up with his books (get him all kinds of books) and his typewriter and his Bible. Slam him down on his knees before texts, broken hearts, and the flippant lives of a superficial flock, and the Holy God. Throw him into the ring to box with God till he learns how short his arms are: engage him to wrestle with God all the night through. Let him come out only when he's bruised and beaten into being a blessing ... Wreck his emotional poise with worry for God, and make him exchange his pious stance for a humble walk with God and man. Make him spend and be spent for the glory of God.
>
> Rip out his telephone, burn up his ecclesiastical success sheets, refuse his glad hand, and put water in the gas tank of his community buggy. Give him a Bible and tie him to the pulpit and make him preach the Word of the Living God.[7]

Oh, that we were men so devoted to prayer that nothing else mattered!

Sober-Minded

The second obstacle to prayer that Peter highlights is a failure to take seriously the practice and the power of prayer. To be sober-minded is to be freed from the world's intoxications and gripped by the sobering realities of God and his kingdom. Peter has just mentioned a sobering reality before he calls us to pray, reminding us that "the end of all things is at hand; therefore be ... sober-minded" (1 Peter 4:7 ESV).

We live in a culture that laughs at evil and is increasingly shallow and ill-equipped to appreciate the truth of God. Truth should lead to sober-minded action. But in many cases, our minds are filled with entertainment, and we take the things of God lightly. The second coming of Christ, the final judgment, the vindication of the crucified Messiah, the eternal glory of the saints, the eternal misery of the damned—these truths ought to wipe the proverbial smirk off our faces. They ought to fill us with a holy gravitas. They ought to move us to pray.

The world around us certainly does not encourage sober-mindedness. The laugh tracks behind our TV sitcoms encourage us to laugh at things that ought to make us weep. On the other hand, our media outlets take themselves very seriously. They portray wars and health epidemics as matters of life and death, and scandalous crimes as being of utmost concern, yet there is no mention of sin, righteousness, and God's judgment. The result is a North American culture that laughs at sin and frets anxiously in the face of the world's instability. But frivolity and anxiety aren't the friends of prayer.

Brothers, if we are to be sober-minded, we must fill our minds with the great truths of Scripture. While we must take seriously the challenges and struggles we face, we must be infinitely more gripped with the reality of the day of the Lord (see Isaiah 2:12; Amos 5:18; 2 Peter 3:10; etc.). We must put off the frivolity of the world, which laughs its head off at moral filthiness, foolish talk, and crude joking (Ephesians 5:4). We must not allow ourselves to laugh at sin, but instead we must be sobered by the fact that a great day of reckoning is coming; for "of this [we] can be sure: No immoral, impure or greedy person—such a person is an idolater—has any inheritance in the kingdom of Christ and of God" (5:5). Let these words pass over us soberly. The Bible is clear that those who live in a pattern of sin and disobedience, both in the world and in the church, will not inherit the glories of heaven. They will be righteously tormented by the severe wrath of God in the eternal blaze of hell. Far from a reason to laugh or joke, this should result in closed mouths and in knees that are bowed in prayer for our people, our neighbors, and our world.

The apostle Paul's prayers were full of sober-minded passion. Remember his testimony in his letter to the Romans: "I have great sorrow and unceasing anguish in my heart. For I could wish that I myself were cursed and cut off from Christ for the sake of my people, those of my own race, the people of Israel" (Romans 9:2–4). The former persecutor of Christians (Acts 8:3, 9:1) was willing to go to hell so his fellow Jews wouldn't have to. He was weeping about their condemnation.

We hear more about this in Romans 10: "Brothers and sisters, my heart's desire and prayer to God for the Israelites is that they may be saved. For I can testify about them that they are zealous for God, but their zeal is not based on knowledge" (verses 1−2). Do you hear this man? He's gripped by the depth of the reality of what it means not to be saved. He realizes that since his fellow Jews don't have the knowledge of God, they'll feel the beating of the wrath of God on their souls forever. Paul is sober-minded about them. No frivolity moved him to make light of the situation. Rather, spiritual and eternal realities gripped his heart and therefore moved him to pray.

In the second half of this book, we will focus on some practical ways to pray for people, and I trust these will help you. But as you move into application and begin setting rhythms and establishing habits of prayer, don't forget that these routines will not help you unless you have faced these obstacles head-on. If we will not walk in holiness in our relationships with God and others—and especially in our marriage relationship—then our prayers will never get off the ground. If we do not exercise self-control, we'll never find the time to pray. And if we don't allow our minds to be sobered by the truth of God's word, our souls will not find the motivation to press on in prayer that is pleasing to God.

I long for you to grow in prayer and to see God move mountains in your church in answer to your prayers. So listen to Jesus when he tells you to gouge out your eyes and cut off your hands to kill sin in your life (Matthew 5:29−30). He knows we are engaging in warfare—that we are fighting our own sins—and we struggle with the world and with the demonic powers that seek to defeat us.

Our great King calls us to exercise self-control. He is able to conquer our distracting lusts by the power of his Spirit. As he does so, we'll find ourselves growing and maturing in our prayer lives.

And never forget that our wonderful and sacrificial Shepherd (John 10:16) has died for us. He has paid the price for all of our wicked sin. He has delivered us from the guilt of sin and will keep us safe from his awful "coming wrath" (1 Thessalonians 1:10). Let these truths fill us with a sober joy that orients our hearts toward prayer.

PART 2

THE PRACTICE
OF PRAYER

Brian Croft

CHAPTER 7

PRAY DELIBERATELY
Intentional Prayer for Each Person

SCRIPTURE TELLS US we will give an account for each soul in our care (Hebrews 13:17). Yet when it comes to prayer, the squeaky wheel often gets the grease. We have a tendency to gravitate to either those we love to be with the most or those who make the most racket and demand our attention. Unintentionally, some church members slip through the cracks.

When I saw this happen in the early years of my ministry, I came up with a deliberate system to remind me to pray for my people.[8] It has become an effective way for me to care for folks and to cut down on unintentional neglect. It's not complicated either. I simply created a prayer guide, which is essentially a booklet with each member of the church listed and the names broken up into a twenty-eight-day chart in alphabetical order. This list needs to represent the realistic, active membership roll of the church.[9] This prayer calendar represents the first twenty-eight days of each month. On day one, I pray for four to five people or family units. After praying for them, I try to make personal contact in the form of a home visit, email, handwritten card, phone call, Facebook note, or text message to let them know I prayed for them on that day. In that moment of personal contact, I try to ask if there is anything I can do to serve them. For those I haven't seen recently, I will usually give them a call or schedule a visit to get an update on how they're doing in general.

I repeat this process for day two, then day three, and all the way to day twenty-eight. If I am faithful and consistent in this process (which I never do perfectly), I will have prayed and made contact in one month with everyone entrusted to my care. On the extra days of the month, I use this process with our missionaries and others we've sent out into ministry. This has become such a fruitful system to help me keep up with our members that I have encouraged our other pastors to use it. As time has gone on, we made a prayer guide for our members as well and encouraged them to begin praying for each other. Several of our members have adopted this model and now also contact folks on the day they pray for them. We've seen amazing fruit from this! It's wonderful to see members taking prayer seriously, praying for one another's needs, and embracing the priesthood of all believers (1 Peter 2:9).

At one of our women's retreats, a dear woman in the church led a project to take our chart and transfer it to index cards that can sit on the table in the form of a flip calendar. Each morning, as they flip to the next day, our members can see the people they need to pray for that day. We do this in our home, and our children make an assertive effort to pray for the names indicated for that day. They even fight over who gets to flip the card. I've been grateful for and encouraged by our church's response to pray for each other—and all it took was providing a simple and deliberate way to accomplish it. We may never know until we are with the Lord all the blessings that have come from this prayer guide. It has created a system of accountability for me and the rest of the pastors, helping us make sure we are deliberately praying for every soul in our flock.

Some pastors have heard me share this and have asked, "Can you do this in a larger church?" In a large church, it's probably too much to expect a single staff member to do this, as others must shepherd and pray as well. However, after spending time on staff at two different churches, each with more than fifteen hundred members, I am convinced that every member can still be cared for, known, and prayed for individually by the pastors and leaders. It is possible to have some form of contact for *each* member *each* month; it just takes wisdom and creative thinking. The twenty-eight-day chart can be used with a ratio of 1 to 100 in larger settings (one pastor/elder/staff is assigned to every one hundred members of the church). This breaks down to fewer than five people or families a day that need to be prayed for and contacted. A five-hundred-member church only needs five shepherds who are willing to put in about thirty minutes a day to accomplish this. A twelve-hundred-member church only needs twelve shepherds to pray for and contact every member.

Yes, all of this takes work. You have to be deliberate and intentional, or it will not happen. You won't stumble into this kind of deliberate effort, regardless of how small or large the church. In fact, you may need to change the way your staff is set up and carries out its work to achieve this. But if you make the commitment to shepherd and pray for every member, I can guarantee that your joy will increase and your people will feel more faithfully cared for by their pastors (Hebrews 13:17).

CHAPTER 8

PRAY PUBLICLY
Corporate Prayer in Public Gatherings

MOST CHRISTIAN CHURCHES have some type of corporate or congregational prayer in their public gatherings.[10] Sadly, many of these "public" prayers tend to be general and generic, or they focus on needs outside the local church. Or maybe your church has the opposite problem, and your public prayers are made up of a list of never-ending requests and superficial needs. They have become routine, lacking genuine, heartfelt concern. Public worship is probably not the time to pray for the recovery of Aunt Millie's dog—especially when Aunt Millie isn't even a member of the church! When pastors fail to pray during their weekly public gatherings, they miss a huge opportunity to model for their members how to pray for one another.

A pastoral prayer in the service allows us to pray about biblical burdens. It is the perfect time to show people how the Bible can guide our prayers. For example, we can loosely follow the model of the Lord's Prayer, asking God to help us acknowledge his holiness, to bring in his kingdom, to accomplish his will in our lives, to provide for our needs, to forgive us our sins, to lead us away from temptation, and to deliver us from evil (Matthew 6:9–13). We can also follow the example of one of Paul's prayers, asking God for "the Spirit of wisdom and revelation, so that [we] may know him better" (Ephesians 1:17). We could spend months praying through different prayers in the Bible. By following these prayers, not only do we model biblical prayer for our people, but we also can increase our confidence—and theirs—that our prayers will be heard since our intercession is fully in line with God's word. Why not begin by saturating your Sunday morning with the biblical promises and prayers we have used in this book?

A pastoral prayer in a service is also a great time to pray for specific needs. This is a time to pray for *specific* people in the church, especially those who are sick and suffering. Try to avoid just praying for general categories like "sick people" or "those who are struggling." Be specific and mention people by name. Appropriate issues include acknowledging recent marriages and births, parenting-related challenges, battles with sin, ways to encourage growth in discipleship, evangelistic opportunities, wisdom for church leaders, and prayers of blessing and empowerment for those who have gone out to engage in ministry or mission work.

Pastoral prayers can be tailored to fit specific occasions. For example, in our church on the nearest Sunday to Veteran's Day, we pray for all who serve in the military, including any who are members of our congregation. Other holidays such as Mother's Day, Memorial Day, Father's Day, the Fourth of July, and Labor Day provide opportunities for special prayers. It's also important to offer pastoral prayers during difficult times in our communities, cities, and nation when tragedies strike and people are hurt, confused, and frightened. Any event or occasion significant in the life of a nation, community, or congregation is an appropriate prayer concern. Many denominations recommend to their churches matters for public prayer. For example, my denomination observes "Sanctity of Human Life Sunday" and "Racial Reconciliation Sunday," just to name two special emphases.[11]

Praying for these needs publicly also helps the congregation be aware of what is happening in the life of the church and community and allows the pastors to model how the congregation can spiritually understand these issues and pray for these needs. Specific, meaningful prayer concerns should be chosen wisely and carefully, and you may need to first seek permission in certain circumstances. The topics mentioned are by no means the only ones you should cover in a public worship service. Whatever is prayed for publicly is highlighted as something important and valuable, and in the long term, it can lead to a congregational prayer ministry that involves the entire congregation.

It is also beneficial for pastors to pray for evangelistic efforts in the community (Colossians 4:3), for other local churches (Ephesians 1:15–16), for our governmental leaders (1 Timothy 2:1–2), and for mission efforts supported by the church (1 Corinthians 16:9). In addition to lifting up the needs of the community and the mission of the church, these prayers inform church members and model how to pray for others. It reminds them of ways the Lord may want to use them to take the gospel to others. These public prayers can motivate your flock to engage in broader kingdom work as salt and light in the world. A pastor who prays for these things will strengthen the hands of his people as they go into the world to minister to others.

Though we've mentioned several appropriate topics for pastoral prayer, some people find that incorporating a specific structure is helpful as well. At our church, we typically precede the pastoral prayer with a reading from Scripture. The prayer opens with some aspect reflected from that reading. This opening can be followed by an element of confession, which may include acknowledgment of our tendency to complain because we aren't content, to form cliques and foster dissension, to be consumed with lust, and, in our Western context, to forget to be thankful for the bounty of living in America. Such a prayer of confession for the sins of the people is modeled by Daniel, who acknowledges, "We have sinned and done wrong. We have been wicked and have rebelled ... We have not listened to your servants the prophets" (Daniel 9:5–6).

Confession can be followed by pleas that God will meet our spiritual and physical needs. Several examples have already been mentioned. Others include prayers for a greater trust in Christ, for government leaders, and for a deeper spiritual brokenness over sin.

Prayers for another church often follow—sometimes for a church pastored by someone ordained out of our church, and other times for another church with whom we share a close sense of fellowship or a church undergoing a particular trial. Prayers for faithfulness to the gospel and unity among believers can be included here. We may also include prayer for a specific missionary here. Often the prayer is for a missionary who has gone out from our congregation, but it doesn't have to be. The main thing to note is that our prayers are for specific churches, specific pastors, specific missionaries, and specific people.

We frequently close our pastoral prayers with requests for the corporate worship gathering we are involved in at that moment. We pray that our singing will be pleasing to God, that our prayers will come before him as a sweet sacrifice, and that the reading and proclamation of God's word will result in glory to Jesus Christ that redounds to God the Father. Remember, this is one suggested structure. Each pastor should adopt a structure that will best benefit his people.

Recommending a structure may raise a question for some readers: Does this imply that prayers are written out beforehand? The short answer is yes, it may mean that. In reality what it means is some planning should take place before one prays in corporate worship. For example, it is edifying to incorporate the language of Scripture into corporate prayers. For some people, all they need to know is the prayer concern, e.g., a specific missionary, and they can readily respond with the memorized words of 1 Corinthians 16:9: "Father, open before them a great door for effective work that your gospel might bear fruit among the people there." Others may need to give more thought to which passages of Scripture are appropriate. Thus, some can pray well extemporaneously. But I suspect these people are the minority. The rest of us should adequately prepare before we pray, some with an outline, others with a written-out prayer. This does not mean your prayer is less sincere or less heartfelt, any more than preparing your sermon ahead of time makes it less sincere or heartfelt.[12]

You may also want to consider leading times of public prayer when the congregation prays for each other. A few years ago, we made a wonderful adjustment to our Sunday evening service so we now spend at least half of our gathering time in prayer. A pastor always leads this time, but he leads by calling on church members to pray for specific needs. The pastor chooses the need that will be prayed for and then calls on someone to pray for that need (a person we've determined will be comfortable praying in front of others). This involves others in the congregation as they pray for one another. Church members do not prepare. They pray a heartfelt prayer for that need. We believe encouraging and equipping the body to publicly pray for one another is an important aspect of leading in prayer. We do this in our evening service because it fits best there, but there's no reason this approach can't be tailored to fit into your specific context.

Pastor, pray for your flock publicly in a way that models how to pray and reminds them that they belong to the Lord, that he is the one who meets their needs. Your leadership is key in teaching them how to pray for each other and for the world around us, and they will experience firsthand your love for them as you intercede in front of them and others on their behalf.

CHAPTER 9

PRAY PASTORALLY
Praying with Fellow Pastors

WHILE IT IS essential for a pastor to develop a personal prayer life, bringing his own needs and the needs of the church before the Lord, prayer is not something we do in isolation. I know from personal experience that the soft voice beckoning pastors to pray for their flocks grows louder when others are involved.[13] Praying with others stirs our faith, encourages us to continue when we grow weary, and provides accountability. I will admit I would have faltered many times if not for the accountability and support of other pastors. With this in mind, I recommend that you schedule monthly or even weekly times to gather with other pastors, with deacons, or with other church leaders to pray for the flock. Set aside times to gather *for the sole purpose* of praying for the needs of people. There are no other agendas, just prayer. You can start with a simple twenty- to thirty-minute time early in the morning before work or school. Pick a time, and then call your leaders and make this a priority. You will quickly learn who has a deep desire in their heart to gather with others to pray.

Pray for the Flock

Another important way to facilitate praying for the flock with others is to use the meetings you've already scheduled. Reserve the first ten to fifteen minutes for prayer. Pastors' meetings, deacons' meetings, small group gatherings, pastoral interns' meetings, staff meetings, and committee meetings are great opportunities to seize. Make this more than just a typical "opening prayer" of a few minutes in length. When you first incorporate this prayer time into your meetings, let people know why you are doing it and what you're hoping to achieve. Then seek to involve others as you pray for specific needs and dedicate a longer time to interceding for the church.

At our church, the pastors gather for a four-hour pastors' meeting once a month on Sunday afternoons. We use half of the time to go through the prayer guide mentioned in chapter 7. As we think about each person on the list, our pastors provide input about what is going on in that member's life. This update time is invaluable because it allows us to be in sync with the needs of the church, thus informing our conversations with these members and helping us pray for them with greater insight and understanding. Once our update time is done, we pray for every person on the list. We have sometimes chosen to discuss and pray for a third of our list, which allows us to spend more focused time on individual church members. The point is, you'll want to take a manageably sized group of your congregation. For some, it will be the entire church membership; for others, it will be a much smaller group.

While we know there are always more issues to discuss, and we've been tempted to steal some of this precious prayer time for business discussions, I'm grateful for our other pastors, who hold me accountable and won't allow me to squeeze out that time. They share the same burden I have to give regular time to pray for our flock.

Fellowship with other pastors outside your own local church is also helpful. Pastors need friendships with others who share their burdens and understand their unique calling. For many pastors, it has to be someone outside their church, because the burdens often involve people in their congregation. Because these situations require confidentiality, we need to be able to seek support from someone who is at a distance from the situations and concerns we are dealing with. Very often, this is a pastor from outside your own church. Pastors need wisdom and counsel from those outside their church to get fresh perspective. Pastors need to coordinate ministry efforts with other pastors and churches to utilize resources and partner together to reach the lost for Christ.

But perhaps the most important reason for pastoral fellowship is the unique way God works when pastors come together from different churches and ministries to pray together for their individual flocks. We started a pastoral fellowship in our city several years ago and now have more than one hundred pastors involved in this group and meeting every other month. One of our most meaningful meetings included a fast from our typical lunch and teaching time and a time of simply praying together for a couple of hours. Each pastor brought great burdens from their own congregations for which they requested prayer from their brothers. What a special, precious time we had as we listened to pastors pray for the burdens of other pastors.

Pray for the Flock

At a recent meeting, one pastor told of a difficult situation in his church—the plight of a single mother with several kids, one of whom was recently diagnosed, at thirteen years of age, with terminal brain cancer. The burden this pastor carries for this family is immense and he is bearing it well. The other pastors in attendance would not have known how to pray for this struggling and weary family or this faithfully serving pastor had it not been for this planned gathering of pastors. Often, only another pastor knows and appreciates the full weight of the burdens being carried.

The technology available today removes some of the geographical barriers that limited the generations before us. At the church I serve, we ordained several men who have gone out to serve as pastors and missionaries, most at great distance from us. With technology such as Skype, we have available the means by which we can look each other in the eye and have real-time conversations about one another's burdens. Many times I have prayed with a brother in England or Africa or several states away, at no cost but our time. Take advantage of these gifts to encourage and pray for and with one another.

Pastor, pray for your flock with other pastors and leaders in your own church, as well as with those from other churches around you. You will find that God will stir your soul uniquely through the joint intercession of this band of brothers.

CHAPTER 10

PRAY GLOBALLY
Praying beyond Your Local Church

IF GOD ANSWERED every prayer you've offered over the past thirty days, what would happen? What would be different about your life, your family, your congregation, and your community? More to the point, would *anything* be different outside of your personal circle of relationships and your local church? Would the world even notice?

Most of us are wired in such a way that we tend to forget about the rest of the world. The tyranny of the urgent overwhelms us. We focus on the people and the tasks that are right before us, demanding our attention. We get consumed with our own circle of life, and we forget there is a world all around us. We forget that God's plan is to redeem the world for himself, and that this plan reaches far beyond our home, our church, and even our city. That's why we need to regularly ask ourselves and our churches, "Are we praying for those outside of our flock? Do we have a sense of God's global work? Are we tuned in to God's plan for the world?"

The local church is the starting point for the Great

Commission. Pastors preach, train, and disciple in the hope that some within their own flock will go out from the church to the world. The story of redemption ends with those from every nation, tribe, language, and people at the throne of grace worshiping Jesus our King. This means that some from the flock *must* be sent to the nations.

But this will be costly. We will lose people we love. If we send out our best, it will require a selfless, kingdom mind-set. No pastor wants to lose the people he cares about, the disciples and leaders he has invested in. No shepherd desires to lose beloved sheep. But this is what we are called to do. And that is why we must pray that God will use our people to fulfill the commission to reach the nations.

Begin by asking for wisdom to identify those who might be called to go, and pray that God moves in the hearts of those who are supposed to be sent. Once you've identified someone, recommend to this person to consider going on a short-term mission trip. The Lord has started a burning passion in the heart of many future missionaries by giving them a taste of what he is doing abroad. It is a sad but joyful experience to love, nurture, raise up, and send one from your flock. But sending them out does not mean they are forgotten. Those sent out become an enduring focus of prayer for you and your church from that moment on.

We have the privilege in our church of having commissioned a missionary to Africa. While on the field, this missionary and his family maintained their membership in our church. Thus, in using our prayer guide mentioned in chapter 7, we prayed for their family monthly when their day came up, just as we do for all the other members. This was a striking monthly reminder that we have brothers and sisters around the globe serving the Lord for the cause of the gospel. Additionally, their names were included in the list of missionaries on one of the days at the end of the month so we were praying for them twice a month.

This same missionary family came home on furlough after several years abroad. They returned to Louisville for their time in the states and plugged back in to the life of our local congregation. They were able to share their experiences on the mission field and were well cared for by our people. Old relationships were renewed, including the friendships between our children and theirs. Now that they have returned to Africa, our children correspond via email and Skype, have a greater appreciation for the Lord's work through this missionary family, and never fail to pray for them. Not every church has this sort of opportunity. But every church can pray for such an opportunity. Additionally, every church can seek out missionaries on furlough to speak to their congregation, inspiring members to pray for them and possibly even answer the call to take the gospel globally.

One last note about praying for God's work in the gospel abroad. The most edifying reading a believer can do, second only to the Bible, is Christian biography, and missionary biographies in particular. The testimonies of how *The Life and Diary of David Brainerd* by Jonathan Edwards has transformed lives are innumerable. The life of John Paton, rightly nicknamed "king of the cannibals," has planted the seed for missions in the heart of many a believer. Biographies like these inspire Christians, not only to holy living and love for God, but also to praying for missionaries they know.

Pray also for your people to impact their neighbors and your city with the gospel. Not all of the people you send can be sent to unreached peoples in distant lands. Some will remain closer to you and invest in ministry outside your local church. A pastor should pray for and encourage his flock to look beyond their church and its programs and ministries. As you pray, encourage your people to get involved with the church's evangelistic efforts in the community. Pray publicly for those ministries you support and carry out in the schools and neighborhoods. Perhaps some of your members are called to help with clothing drives or to work with the homeless or to serve at orphan care centers. Others may have a passion to serve at crisis pregnancy centers or do street preaching on the weekends. Pray about and then encourage these forms of involvement. It will help your people learn how to step out of that comfortable place in the church where many try to hide.

Pray for your people to be mindful of suffering Christians around the world. Spend time introducing them to Christians who are persecuted for their faith. It's easy for American Christians to lose sight of the suffering and persecution that still exists in the world as we enjoy our free and flourishing lifestyles. Pray for your flock to engage in ministries that serve these suffering people and challenge them to get involved.

Pray for the missionaries you actively support and for the other local churches in your area. Most Sunday mornings, our pastoral prayer includes petitions for another local church, as well as for one of our missionaries on the field. Keeping these needs and concerns before your church members in a public way not only shows them how to pray; it encourages unity with other churches and provides a needed reminder that the kingdom of God and the glory of Christ extend far beyond our own church and personal lives. Because we are wired to forget the world, we should use our prayers for our flock to nudge them to engage with the universal church and learn to expand their vision of what God can and will do.

Pastor, pray that God raises up people who serve beyond the walls of your local church. Pray that they remember their brothers and sisters down the road and throughout the world who are suffering as they serve the Savior. And in your prayers, call out some who might be called to leave your church to serve in another town or even in another country. While it's painful to say good-bye, there is nothing more exciting than seeing God work in this way in your midst. It's worth the cost.

CHAPTER 11

PRAY SACRIFICIALLY
Combining Prayer with Fasting

I MUST CONFESS that I (Brian) do not have much experience with fasting. My coauthor and colleague, Ryan, has probably fasted more days during the writing of this book than I have during my entire life. But in some ways, it is my lack of discipline in this area that is the reason I'm writing this chapter and not Ryan. Why do I say that?

I'm going to assume most of you are like me. You've heard others talk about fasting. You affirm the validity of fasting today and may even encourage your flock to fast. Yet when it comes to fasting as a regular discipline, you fall short.

In this chapter, my goal is to encourage you, not as one who has this discipline down pat, but as one who struggles and is still growing in this practice. Fasting, when combined with the practice of prayer, is a powerful tool God uses to increase our desire for him and to focus our prayers for greater effectiveness.

A basic definition of fasting is "the withholding of food for a certain amount of time for the sake of creating a more disciplined and earnest attitude of prayer." How does this work? The simplest way to explain it is to say that the moments we inevitably feel unfulfilled hunger pains of food should instead move us to pray. We translate our natural hunger for food, which is necessary for life, into prayer. Our physical yearnings are transferred into spiritual hunger for God, for the life we have in him, and for him to do what only he can do.

Consider these two simple guidelines if you are new to fasting. First, a fast doesn't always have a particular time limit on it or specific rules you must follow about what to give up. You can fast for a day or for a month. You can do a water-only or a juice-only fast. You can fast one meal once a week or one full day every month. You can abstain from certain foods like desserts, and when you feel the urge to reach for a cookie, your desire can be channeled into an urgency to pray. There are no rules. Do what will create in you a greater urgency and hunger to pray.

Second, be mindful of any health issues that could make a fast unwise. For example, if you are a diabetic or have any other physical condition that requires a strict diet, be especially mindful not to put yourself in a compromised position as a result of a fast. I also discourage the idea of fasting for those who struggle with eating disorders that are making intake of food a challenge and concern in their daily living. The point of the fast is to combine it with a more intense, focused time of prayer that brings a greater communion with God, a greater empowerment of the Spirit, and a greater earnestness in your soul.

Here are several occasions on which a pastor should fast and pray—specifically for those in his flock:

Pray for the Flock

1. Fast as you seek direction and vision for the church in a key transition time. Local churches go through seasons of transition, and these times can prove to be pivotal in the life of a church. Members move away. Conversions happen. Staff members come and go. Conflicts arise and difficulties come. Suffering is inevitable. Leadership structure changes are made. Try to discern these key transitions, and set time aside to fast and pray to seek God's wisdom on those matters.

2. Fast when you desire a greater sense of the Holy Spirit's work in your preaching ministry. Yes, we should always desire the Spirit's presence. However, preachers can get in ruts. There are moments when we feel a particular dryness in our soul and become burdened with the neediness of the congregation for God's presence to be more apparent. Fasting can be a helpful way to press through the rut and invite a fresh move of the Spirit in your life and in the life of the church.

3. Fast when a great provision for the congregation is needed and a deadline is looming. This could be related to the church as it faces a great financial hurdle, or to certain church members who struggle with the basic provisions of food and shelter. Fast and pray for specific provisions, believing God can provide and will do so according to his will. Fasting affirms the urgency of the need and hopefully the earnestness of your prayers for God to supernaturally provide for your people.

4. Fast when the congregation appears to be suffering in serious, unique ways. Several years ago, I went through a month when three key church members died, one in a tragic car wreck that left behind a wife and two little kids. I didn't fast in that season, but I should have. God was kind to care for us, but I believe a focused time of prayer through fasting would have been fruitful in light of the unique moment of suffering that had come on all of us in our church in an unusually challenging way.

5. *Fast when you experience a season of numeric growth.* We often forget to pray when we flourish, but it is just as essential to do so then as during seasons of leanness. Fasting and prayer during seasons of growth can provide a focus of reliance on Christ when we are tempted to rely on ourselves. Prayer can act as the great equalizer that takes us to the foot of the cross and reminds us Christ is building his church, not us. This time of prayer for our people can also give us wisdom in how to best care for our church, as well as for those who come in as new members.

6. *Fast when you sense an abnormal amount of spiritual attack on the congregation.* I am profoundly guilty of losing sight of the spiritual battle that is being waged in our midst. The sacrifice and intensity that fasting brings can heighten our awareness of these spiritual realities we are tempted to ignore.

7. *Fast when certain sheep go astray and won't come back.* Nothing breaks the heart of a shepherd like seeing sheep go astray. Oftentimes, pastors are left asking what more they can do to bring them back. At some point, we must do what we can to pursue them, but then surrender them to God, knowing he is the only one who can bring them back. Fasting can be a focused guide for our surrendering control over the situation to the Lord, who has the power to bring back those who belong to him. Prayer can also be a helpful way to gain wisdom on how to pursue those who are wayward.

Pray for the Flock

You know you should be praying for your flock regularly. But there are special moments and urgent needs and circumstances that demand our attention. In these times, consider dedicating time to fasting in combination with praying. Trust God to use your fast to increase your focus in prayer. Sacrifice food and time in the discipline of fasting so God might meet with you in a sweet, unusual way to minister to your soul and the souls of your flock through you.

CHAPTER 12

PRAY OCCASIONALLY
Praying at Special Occasions

IT WAS A cold Minnesota afternoon. My wife's family had gathered to celebrate the life of her grandmother, who had recently died, six months after her one hundredth birthday. As a pastor, I'm used to people asking me to say a prayer or give a word at a service. But in this case, I was continually assured I was definitely *not* needed to participate at either the funeral or the graveside service. With some relief, I relaxed, grateful to have just one task for the day—caring for my wife. The funeral went just as planned, and we found ourselves standing around the graveside as the day drew to a close. There was an awkward, uncomfortable silence. And at that moment I knew what would happen next. One of the patriarchs of the family looked at me. "Brian, would you say something?"

It's hard in those moments to say no. My car, thankfully, was nearby, and as I went to retrieve my Bible, I had a few moments to think of what I might say. I was aware both Christians and non-Christians were present, so when I returned, I proceeded to read Scripture, share the hope of the gospel, and pray. My words weren't all that profound or overly impressive. But the family was grateful—especially my wife. She had been longing to give her family—these dear, hurting people—a true word about Christ, namely, that death is not the end for those who are in Christ. That graveside service proved to be a key moment, one that ministered to my wife's family in a way I could not have done had they come to hear me preach on a Sunday morning.

There is something special that happens in these unplanned moments. People sense that you care, and God often works in these unplanned times in unexpected, yet powerful ways.

And yet, that's not how we usually feel when they happen. Most of the time, these unplanned requests feel more like an inconvenience. Because they are unplanned, they seem like distractions from our real work. But that just reveals we want to control our ministry. Times like this are a natural part of our calling as pastors. In ministry, you simply cannot plan for every situation that comes up. You cannot prepare for every circumstance.

As a pastor, there will be spontaneous requests for prayer. People will ask you to say a prayer to bless the food at a party, a prayer for a newly married couple at the reception, a prayer at an evangelistic event, a prayer in a hospital when you are casually visiting. You may be invited to the podium to say a closing prayer at a community service you are attending or to offer a prayer at a graveside service you are not leading. These are all special moments when you can minister through prayer by making the gospel known and by specifically praying for the blessing of the people in attendance. Learn to embrace these opportunities and don't just see them as inconveniences to be avoided. They can be a way of caring for your flock.

Still, there are a few hurdles we must learn to overcome. We have to be willing to embrace spontaneity. The planner/control freak in me can easily despise these moments and even consider it rude when I'm called on in this way. But Paul's call to Timothy is a helpful reminder: "Be prepared in season and out of season" (2 Timothy 4:2). This word doesn't just apply to our preaching and evangelism; it's a good word for all of our ministry, including prayer. Learn to trust in God's providence in these moments, and embrace the opportunities he provides.

You also need to let go of your need to impress others. Every public prayer we pray doesn't have to call down the heavens with our hyperarticulate words. Trust in the Spirit to give you the words you need—just the right words for that unique moment. God often powerfully uses what seem to be mediocre prayers in these special occasions because we have no choice but to pray from the overflow of our heart. There is nothing wrong with preparation, but honest prayers like these honor God, and he uses them in ways we don't realize at the time.

Many of these opportunities are not *suddenly* forced on us. We often are asked ahead of time to pray at a wedding or a funeral service. We can overanalyze these special occasions, thinking we have to justify our involvement or make a statement through our prayer. But we need to remember that the prayer is not about us or our agenda. Be flexible. Embrace this as an opportunity to model for your people what it looks like to call on the Lord at this special time. But don't try to make it more than it needs to be. Sometimes the simplest prayers are the best. Call on Jesus. Say a word of blessing. Thank the Lord for his kindness. Remember the good news of the gospel.

An invitation to pray is always good, so don't waste it. Special occasions may seem inconvenient or even risky, depending on the circumstances, but learn to embrace the risk. Pray real, honest, powerful words of truth about Jesus and his word. Pray specifically for your people when appropriate. And model for them *how* to pray on these special occasions.

CONCLUSION
Brian Croft

CHRISTIAN PASTORS HAVE been given a great gift, namely, the ability to intercede for the needs of their flock through the mediating work of Jesus and the presence of the Holy Spirit. As pastors, we are not called to be the intercessor and mediator who reconciles our people to God. That work has already been fully and completely accomplished in the life, death, and resurrection of Jesus Christ. Jesus now reigns at the right hand of God, interceding for all who have trusted in Christ and been transformed by the gospel. Our calling is to cry out to the one who intercedes for us. We bring the needs of God's people to the Chief Shepherd. We lead others by our example. We gather God's people and corporately bring the needs and concerns of the church before the Lord. This is part of our work as shepherds and as pastors. What better way to shepherd God's people than to go to our Father and plead for them in the name of Jesus?

Hopefully, we have convinced you of the importance of prayer in your ministry to your flock. The words of the great nineteenth-century Baptist pastor Charles Spurgeon serve as an appropriate warning to each of us if we fail to make prayer a central foundation of our work as a pastor:

Pray for the Flock

The preacher who neglects to pray much must be very careless about his ministry. He cannot have comprehended his calling. He cannot have computed the value of a soul, or estimated the meaning of eternity. He must be a mere official, tempted into a pulpit because the piece of bread which belongs to the priest's office is very necessary to him, or a detestable hypocrite who loves the praise of men, and cares not for the praise of God. He will surely become a mere superficial talker, best approved where grace is least valued and a vain show most admired. He cannot be one of those who plough deep and reap abundant harvests. He is a mere loiterer, not a labourer. As a preacher he has a name to live and is dead. He limps in his life like the lame man in the Proverbs, whose legs were not equal, for his praying is shorter than his preaching.[14]

Take these words to heart. I know I've done so in my own life and ministry. And may the Chief Shepherd move in you, as the shepherd of his flock, to keep you from falling into a superficial, prayerless ministry. When you sense the desire to pray, respond quickly to that soft voice in your heart. Over time, you will learn to develop a habit of prayer, and prayer will become a greater priority in your life. Create daily disciplines that systematically enable you to pray for all of your people. And involve others in this work, rejoicing together that you have full access to God because of the perfect mediating work of our Redeemer and Savior, Jesus Christ. To him be the glory forever!

ACKNOWLEDGMENTS

RYAN WOULD LIKE TO THANK ...

My God! I am thankful to my Father for choosing me for salvation and sending his Son to save me. I am also deeply thankful that instead of allowing me to continue on a path of lying, promiscuity, and drug abuse, he saved me and gave me the high and holy calling of being a vocational minister of the gospel. I am very thankful that on the way to heaven, he has also given me the opportunity to write this book. Thank you, Father!

My parents and stepparents, who have each sacrificed to raise me. As I write my first book, I am specifically thankful to my mother, Pam Collins, who refused to follow her own dreams until she had seen her high school dropout son finally finish high school. Thanks, Mom! I cudda never dun it without u.

Brian Croft, for giving me the opportunity to write with him. For more than ten years, Brian has been a friend, a counselor, a colaborer, and example to me. Brother, it is a deep honor to work with a friend like you. Thanks for your patience with me. You have been a great teacher.

The elders, deacons, and congregation of Immanuel Baptist Church. What a privilege it is to be a part of such a praying people. Tears come to my eyes as I think about you and the joy it is to watch God answer prayers through you. I love being your Pastor, Immanuel.

Three generations of Teals. My wife's grandfather, Wilbur Norman Teal, was a pastor, traveling evangelist, and mighty man of faith and prayer. Nothing (outside of the Bible) has spurred me on to value prayer more than the stories of answered prayer from his life. With tears, I thank God for his legacy of faith. I also thank his son, my father-in-law, Grant Dennis Teal, for his example of humility and his timely exhortation. Years ago, Grant told me I needed to know more of the work of the Spirit. He was right—and faithful are the words of a friend. Finally, I want to thank my wife, Christy Fullerton. Through trials, sufferings, and limitations I have seen Christy demonstrate a sweet, clear, and pronounced gift of faith. How many times I have said, "I know something is going to happen, because Christy is praying about it!" As I write these words, I am falling apart in a coffee shop hoping no one will notice the guy on the couch who is fighting off sobs. I love you, Christy Fullerton. I am thankful for you, your faith in God, and your gracious and kind faith that God is actually at work in me.

BRIAN WOULD LIKE TO THANK ...

The faithful folks at Zondervan for believing in this series and what Practical Shepherding exists for. You are a meaningful partner in our effort to care for pastors.

Scott Wells, for your invaluable contribution to this book. Your significant additions, rewrites, and counsel made so much of this book stronger than it would have been otherwise.

Acknowledgments

Don Whitney, for writing the foreword and your kind investment in both Ryan and me throughout the years.

My fellow pastors at Auburndale Baptist Church. It is one of my greatest joys to pray for our flock with you.

The faithful saints at Auburndale Baptist Church. What a gift it is to have you on my mind and heart as I go to our Father in prayer.

My family, as your love, support, and prayers for me are the most meaningful.

Jesus Christ, for saving my soul so I can cry out to you, not just for the flock you entrusted to my care, but for my own needy soul—and you always hear me.

PRAYER GUIDE TEMPLATE

Brian Croft

BELOW IS A template of the prayer guide we use at Auburndale Baptist Church. This guide is designed to help us pray for every member of the church in the course of a month. This is also used by the pastors to keep watch over every soul under our care. The entire membership is divided up through day twenty-eight of the month. During the final two or three days of the month, we pray for missionaries and former members we have sent out into the ministry. The longer version has mailing addresses, email addresses, and phone numbers. The (s) is for "shut-ins" and the (w) is for "widow/widower."

First day of the month
Abner, Jason and Lacey
 Kids: Riley and Carter
Adkins, Ken and Beth

Pray for the Flock

Second day of the month
Ally, Douglas and Cammie
    Kids: Kenneth, expecting #2
Annett, Joe and Lisa
Ash, Ellen (w and s)

Third day of the month
Baker, Michael and Raechel
Bass, Diane (s)
Bell, Luke and Kathy
    Kids: Abby, Jack, and Micah

Fourth day of the month
Bolton, Dave and Sally
Carey, Pete and Laura
    Kids: Expecting #1

Fifth day of the month
Carmack, Chuck and Kathy
Cheatham, Don and Carrie
    Kids: Dawn and Alice

This continues through day twenty-eight . . .

REFLECTIONS ON MY FORTY-DAY FAST

Ryan Fullerton

RECENTLY, GOD LED me to pray and fast for forty days.

I feel a little funny writing this because fasting is something that is often done in secret (Matthew 6:16–18). However, not all fasts must be done in secret (Acts 13:1–3). And some fasts *cannot* be done in secret. When you pass up one meal, it's possible that no one will ask questions. But when you pass up 120 meals, people notice. When you lose thirty pounds, people start to ask questions. Fasting for forty days can be done Godwardly, but it would be hard to do secretly.

Because it's no secret that I've been fasting, I want to share some thoughts about what it's been like for me. I hope my experience will stir up in you a revival of seeking the Lord through prayer and fasting.

DISCLAIMER: Before you choose to fast, it'd be wise to seek sufficient counsel from the Bible, fellow Christians, pastors, and perhaps even from a medical doctor.

Pray for the Flock

1. Not everyone should fast for forty days. Forty-day fasts are rare in the Bible. Moses fasted for forty days and forty nights during the giving of the law on Mount Sinai (Exodus 34:28; Deuteronomy 9:9). And he did it again after he found Israel breaking the law by worshiping the golden calf (Deuteronomy 9:18). Elijah fasted for forty days as well (1 Kings 19:7–8). And Jesus began his earthly ministry by fasting for forty days (Matthew 4:2). Moses, Elijah, Jesus. Three people in the Bible. That's it. Not everyone should fast for forty days and forty nights.

2. Everyone should fast. During his teaching ministry, Jesus did not say "if you fast," but "when you fast." He assumes we will fast and tells us how (Matthew 6:16–17). No one who wants to grow in Christ should neglect the gift of going with less so you can seek God more.

3. Not all fasting is the same. Moses did not eat or drink (Deuteronomy 9:9, 18). (Don't try this at home. This is deadly unless God is miraculously sustaining you.) Jesus did not eat (Matthew 4:2). Daniel did not eat delicacies for a season. He gave up meat and wine for three weeks so he could give himself to seeking the Lord (Daniel 10:3). Fasting can be for varying durations and entail giving up different things. A good friend told me yesterday he is not eating dessert for three months so he can seek God's power for a church he is hoping to plant. That's fasting. You don't have to go to the most radical extremes of fasting to make your fasting "real fasting."

4. Not all fasting is good. In Isaiah 58, the people of God have been seeking God with fasting. However, we're told their fasting was not good because they were living in wickedness when they should have been showing mercy. God told them, "Your fasting ends in quarreling and strife, and in striking each other with wicked fists. You cannot fast as you do today and expect your voice to be heard on high" (verse 4). Then he instructed them, "Is not this the kind of fasting I have chosen: to loose the chains of injustice and untie the cords of the yoke, to set the oppressed free and break every yoke? Is it not to share your food with the hungry and to provide the poor wanderer with shelter—when you see the naked, to clothe them, and not to turn away from your own flesh and blood?" (verses 6–7). Fasting that is not accompanied by repentance and obedience is rejected by God. We can pray and fast all night, but if we do not move in obedience, God warns us, "If anyone turns a deaf ear to my instruction, even their prayers are detestable" (Proverbs 28:9).

   5. Not all fasting is good because food is very good. About two weeks into my fast, I casually overheard my daughter say, "I'm going to have a toasted cheese bagel with butter." I thought to myself, *Man, what amazing gifts I often overlook! Toasted cheese bagel with butter!* Nothing about fasting should be a rejection of the goodness of food. God created all food good (Genesis 1), and only demons teach otherwise. In his first letter to Timothy, Paul writes:

> The Spirit clearly says that in later times some will abandon the faith and follow deceiving spirits and things taught by demons. Such teachings come through hypocritical liars, whose consciences have been seared as with a hot iron. They forbid people to marry and order

them to abstain from certain foods, which God created to be received with thanksgiving by those who believe and who know the truth. For everything God created is good, and nothing is to be rejected if it is received with thanksgiving.

1 Timothy 4:1–4

Fasting that runs away from the good gift of food is really running away from God.

6. *Fasting is an intensifier.* Fasting is a way of intensifying our ordinary pursuit of God. In the words of John Piper, fasting says, "This much, O God, I want you."[15]

7. *Fasting can intensify our seeking of God.* In Daniel, we read, "So I turned to the Lord God and pleaded with him in prayer and petition, in fasting, and in sackcloth and ashes" (9:3). Notice he was intensifying his prayer with pleas. He provoked his hunger by fasting and channeled that hunger toward God. He provoked his discomfort with sackcloth and ashes and directed that discomfort toward God. Fasting helps us intensify our seeking of God by redirecting the energies and passions we normally fix on food to the living God.

8. *Fasting can intensify our repentance.* In the book of Joel, God tells his people, "'Even now,' declares the LORD, 'return to me with all your heart, with fasting and weeping and mourning'" (2:12). Fasting accompanies repentance. It belongs in the company of intense actions like weeping and mourning. Fasting reminds us that repentance is not glib or light. Real repentance is like an earthquake upheaval in our souls. Isaiah describes real repentance as a seismic upheaval: "Every valley shall be raised up, every mountain and hill made

low; the rough ground shall become level, the rugged places a plain" (40:4). If your soul needs the upheaval of repentance, then fasting is a great intensifier.

9. Fasting is a fitting response to an intense situation. Sometimes the situation we are in is already intense. In such cases, fasting is the right way to say to God, *I get it!* Wayne Grudem (who has influenced my last three points) writes, "Prayer is often connected with fasting in Scripture. Sometimes these are occasions of intense supplication before God, as ... when the Jews learned of the decree of Ahasuerus that they would all be killed, and 'there was great mourning among the Jews, with *fasting* and weeping and lamenting, and many of them lay in sackcloth and ashes' (Esther 4:3)."[16] In response to the intense threat of genocide, the Jews responded with intense prayer and fasting.

10. Fasting is often mightily used by God. After Moses fasted, God relented from his wrath (Deuteronomy 9:19). When the leaders of the church at Antioch fasted, the Holy Spirit spoke and sent out two of the most powerful apostolic missionaries the world has ever seen (Acts 13:1 – 5). Before God does a mighty work, he often moves in his people to seek his face through prayer and fasting.

11. I needed to fast. For a number of months and years, I have been feeling what the nineteenth-century preacher Octavius Winslow called "personal declension" in my soul. I did not seem to be making progress in my walk with God and my victory over sin. I have felt my time for prayer crowded out. I have felt my conscience grow duller. I have felt my hunger for God grow faint. I looked at the people I pastor, and although

I saw great marks of grace in them, I saw a great need for more of God's Spirit on them. I needed to fast.

12. I was moved to fast for revival. I believe wherever there are true Christians, the Spirit of God is at work. Even when Christians are at their lowest—like when the Corinthians were visiting prostitutes—they are still the people of the Spirit (1 Corinthians 6:19). Having said that, how can we ever be satisfied with such a sad state of affairs? If you are, you are probably not a Christian. Christians were made to be filled with the Spirit, to live by the Spirit, and to repeatedly experience fresh fillings of the empowering Holy Spirit of God (Acts 1:8, 2:4, 4:31; Galatians 5:16; Ephesians 5:18). Christians were meant to drink of the living waters of the Lord Jesus Christ. When they do, they are promised that out of their hearts "rivers of living water will flow" (John 7:38). I was not experiencing that, so I devoted myself to fasting and prayer for a revival of religion in my soul and in God's people.

13. I was moved to fast for repentance. My wife, Christy, and I have seen that there is too much anger in our home. Our home is not a raging volcano of rage. We have a lot of love for one another and our kids. But far too often, it is a place of anger, irritability, and frustration. Despite the plain teachings of the Bible, we seem to believe the lie that the anger of man can produce the righteousness of God (James 1:20). We felt compelled to deal with that issue more severely. We long to commend the gospel to one another and to our children, so we fasted, asking the Lord to forgive us and to change us.

14. I was moved to fast for self-control. I like food. I like it a lot. I don't just like seconds; I like thirds. I like ice cream.

No, I *love* ice cream. I like ice cream too much. Now earlier, I wrote that food is good. I still believe that's true. (For instance, there's a piece of Dairy Queen cake in my freezer right now, and I plan to eat it to the glory of God.) Nevertheless, Peter writes, "The end of all things is at hand; therefore be self-controlled and sober-minded for the sake of your prayers" (1 Peter 4:7 ESV). When you lose self-control, you lose prayer. In my case, too much food made me too sluggish to pray. Food became my comfort in place of my seeking God's consolations in prayer. I needed to gouge out an eye and cut off a hand in my battle against sin (Matthew 5:29–30), so I fasted.

15. I was moved to fast for a building. For more than two years, our church has been praying for a building. During that time, we have seen remarkable answers to prayer. God has surprised us with the amounts of money he has directed our way. It's been marvelous, but it hasn't gotten us a building. Every time we get close to getting a building, our sovereign God moves the building and it slips through our hands. I felt compelled to keep praying. Words like these from the Puritan preacher Jonathan Edwards have moved me to persist in prayer:

> It is very apparent from the word of God, that he is wont often to try the faith and patience of his people, when crying to him for some great and important mercy, by withholding the mercy sought, for a season; and not only so, but at first to cause an increase of dark appearances. And yet he, without fail, at last succeeds those who continue instant in prayer, with all perseverance, and "will not let him go except that he blesses ..."[17]

God blesses those who will not let him go (Genesis 32:26), so I fasted and prayed for a building.

16. I was moved to fast for prayer. For a long time, I have felt like my prayer life needed deepening. I know we will always want to grow in prayer, but I felt especially burdened to grow at this time. God had been giving me so many opportunities—opportunities to lead my wife, to lead my kids, to teach, to write, to lead other pastors, and to lead our growing congregation. All of these opportunities were coming to me, and I was afraid I'd have no way to deal with them faithfully without more prayer. Years ago, I read the autobiography of the Scottish missionary Daniel Smith.[18] In it, he told the story of what happened after he arrived in China. The leader of the China Inland Mission invited him to his room and proceeded to pray over all the missionaries he was responsible for. This lasted for four hours. I've never hit four hours of consecutive prayer. I currently can't imagine praying for four hours daily, but I want to get a lot closer so that everything I do is bathed in prayer and anointed by the Holy Spirit of God.

17. I was moved to fast and pray by Moses. The idea to fast and pray came to me as I was studying to preach from Deuteronomy 9. In this chapter, Moses fasts and prays for forty days—twice. What struck me was that when the people were ensnared in sin, the leader prayed. In thinking about my sin and the sins of the people I pastor, it seemed as though the Lord was laying it on my heart to follow this example.

18. I chose to do a juice fast. I'm the kind of guy who has to remind himself that the most radical is not always the best. I am glad I did in this case. I'm not sure I could have survived on just water. I needed some energy. I had a lighter load this summer, but I was still working and needing energy to do the tasks God gave me to do. For forty days, I drank lots of water and had two to four fruit juices every day. God was kind to bless me with a clear mind and lots of energy. I tried to use that energy wisely by not doing anything physically strenuous during my time of fasting. I took fairly long walks, and that was about it.

19. I let God decide what he would do through my fasting. As I planned to fast for forty days, I was careful to allow the Lord to determine the results. I wanted to avoid a sense of entitlement. I wanted to avoid the kind of thinking that says, *I fasted for forty days. Surely I should have at least one shower of your love.* Or, *I fasted for forty days. Surely we should have a building by now.* When we fast, we are not forcing God's hand or earning God's favor. We are using God's appointed channel of grace to ask him for the things he has graciously promised to give.

20. The Lord has been the Shepherd of my fast. Around thirty days in, I began to get frustrated. I had a sense I wasn't going to get the answers I longed for. Psalm 23 was a great comfort at that time: "The LORD is my shepherd; I shall not want" (Psalm 23:1 ESV). God has promised to give me everything I need. He doesn't always give it to us right away (see the other 149 psalms), but he does meet our needs in his good time. As I struggled, he helped me to rely on that. I felt a sweetness in knowing he is my Shepherd.

21. I was not the hero of my fast. About three days into fasting, I turned to Christy and said something like, "If I make it through this fast, I will not be the hero. Jesus Christ will be the hero." I knew I wouldn't be the hero because on my first day of fasting, I needed a three-hour nap. No coffee + no sugar = no energy. I was done. After that, I kept fasting, but it was still hard to pray. I don't have the passion to achieve a heroic fast. But God gave me grace to just keep seeking him.

22. *Fasting has helped me stay current.* Before my fast, I felt overwhelmed. I felt like I had a thousand really important things to pray about but didn't have the time I needed to pray for them. Fasting helped me to lay out all of my concerns before the Lord repeatedly. I believe I was able to lay out all of my sins, all of my troubles, and all of my desires before the Lord multiple times. It has been great to walk with God in this way.

23. *Fasting has not solved all of my problems.* I have been angry over the course of my forty-day fast. I have battled discouragement. I have not seen a mighty revival. I have wasted time while on my fast (I think I need a total social media fast). Another building we were pursuing slipped through our fingers and into the hands of another owner during my fast. I may be a fasting saint, but I'm still a saint who struggles with sin and stands in constant need of the Mediator's grace and mercy (1 Timothy 2:5).

24. *Fasting has been a wonderful blessing to me.* I've seen victory over anger as I went through my fast. Not full victory, but real and sweet victory. I have not seen a mighty revival, but I have felt reenergized by the Spirit. We haven't received a building yet, but a new and remarkable possibility has opened up, and we are pursuing it right now.

Reflections on My Forty-Day Fast

25. Fasting will be a wonderful blessing to me. I have not seen all the answers to prayer that I desire. But just because I'm done with this season of intense asking does not mean God is done with his season of answering. I trust he will answer all of my prayers. I even trust he will answer most of them with a resounding yes. A few he may have to decline. But I have prayed according to his word. Many times while fasting, I'd try to give a specific verse to back up every request I made, and I know he will answer my prayers in his due time. In the future (near or far), I will see more of the work of God because I sought the Lord with fasting.

I end with these words from John Piper: "Christian fasting, at its root, is the hunger of a homesickness for God."[19]

NOTES

1. John Newton, "Come, My Soul, Thy Suit Prepare," in *Olney Hymns* (London: W. Oliver, 1779).
2. Wayne Grudem, *Systematic Theology: An Introduction to Bible Doctrine* (Grand Rapids: Zondervan, 1994), 332.
3. Maurice Roberts, *The Thought of God* (Edinburgh: Banner of Truth, 1993), 57–58, emphasis added.
4. Thomas Chalmers, "The Expulsive Power of a New Affection," in *The Works of Thomas Chalmers* (New York: Robert Carter, 1830).
5. D. A. Carson, *A Call to Spiritual Reformation: Priorities from Paul and His Prayers* (Grand Rapids: Baker Academic, 1992), 194.
6. Quoted in R. Kent Hughes, *Ephesians: The Mystery of the Body of Christ* (Wheaton, IL: Crossway, 1990), 151.
7. Floyd Doud Shafer, "And Preach as You Go!" *Christianity Today*, March 27, 1961, http://biblicalstudies.info/preacher/doud_preach.htm (accessed February 10, 2015).
8. See appendix 1 for a template to this prayer guide. Note that this chapter summarizes content originally published in Brian Croft, *The Pastor's Ministry* (Grand Rapids: Zondervan, 2015).
9. When I came to our church, hundreds of people on the membership rolls hadn't been involved or even present at a service in many years. Until you can address the problem of a membership that is inaccurate and outdated, create a list of those who are actively involved in the church, as well as those who would be involved if they were physically able to do so (shut-ins). Don't wait for the list to become accurate to pursue this method of prayer and soul care, as membership rolls can take years to reform in an established church.
10. Note that this chapter summarizes content originally published in Brian Croft, *The Pastor's Ministry*.
11. Whatever the situation, remember that occasions like these, though they are most commonly a cause of joy, celebration, and honor, can be a source of pain for others. For example, Mother's Day can be very difficult for the woman who has never been able to bear children. Labor Day can be a reminder of shame for an unemployed member who is striving hard, but unsuccessfully, to get a job. Ask yourself, *Who in my congregation might be negatively affected by this?* and then pray for discernment in your praying.
12. A wonderful resource for planning effective public prayer is Terry L. Johnson and J. Ligon Duncan III, "Recommendations for Improving Public Prayer," 9Marks, February 25, 2010, http://9marks.org/article/recommendations-improving-public-prayer/ (accessed February 10, 2015).

Notes

13. Note that this chapter summarizes content originally published in Brian Croft, *The Pastor's Ministry* (Grand Rapids: Zondervan, 2015).

14. Charles Spurgeon, *Lectures to My Students* (Grand Rapids: Zondervan, 1954), 48.

15. John Piper, *A Hunger for God: Desiring God through Fasting and Prayer* (Wheaton, IL: Crossway, 1997), 23. A free downloadable PDF of the book is available at www.DesiringGod.org/books/a-hunger-for-god.

16. Wayne Grudem, *Systematic Theology: An Introduction to Biblical Doctrine* (Grand Rapids: Zondervan, 1994), 390.

17. Jonathan Edwards, "An Humble Attempt," in *The Works of Jonathan Edwards*, ed. Edward Hickman (1834; Edinburgh: Banner of Truth, 1974), 2:312.

18. Daniel Smith, *Pilgrim of the Heavenly Way: The Autobiography of Daniel Smith, Christian Missionary to Asia* (Hannibal, MO: Granted Ministries, 2010).

19. Piper, *A Hunger for God*, 14.

Practical
Shepherding

Brian Croft, series editor
www.practicalshepherding.com

The Practical Shepherding series provides pastors and ministry leaders with practical help to do the work of pastoral ministry in a local church. The seven-volume series includes:

- *Conduct Gospel-Centered Funerals: Applying the Gospel at the Unique Challenges of Death*

- *Prepare Them to Shepherd: Test, Train, Affirm, and Send the Next Generation of Pastors*

- *Visit the Sick: Ministering God's Grace in Times of Illness*

- *Comfort the Grieving: Ministering God's Grace in Times of Loss*

- *Gather God's People: Understand, Plan, and Lead Worship in Your Local Church*

- *Pray for the Flock: Ministering God's Grace Through Intercession*

- *Oversee God's People: Shepherding the Flock Through Administration and Delegation*

In addition to this series, be sure to look for these titles by Brian and Cara Croft on the pastor's family and ministry:

- *The Pastor's Family: Shepherding Your Family through the Challenges of Pastoral Ministry* by Brian and Cara Croft

- *The Pastor's Ministry: Biblical Priorities for Faithful Shepherds* by Brian Croft